BLITZKRIEG

POLAND
AND SCANDINAVIA
1939 – 1940

WILL FOWLER

Ian Allan

60th
ANNIVERSARY

First published 2002

ISBN 0 7110 2943 1

Published by Ian Allan Publishing
an imprint of Ian Allan Publishing Ltd, Hersham, Surrey KT12 4RG.

Printed by Ian Allan Printing Ltd, Hersham, Surrey KT12 4RG.

Code: 0210/A2

Designed by Casebourne Rose Design Associates Ltd

Illustrations by Mike Rose
Maps by Monty Black

Picture Credits
All photographs are from Bugle Archives.
Page 70 IWM.

COVER PICTURE: The commander of a PzKpfw IV in the distinctive black Panzer uniform.

CONTENTS

BLITZKRIEG

THE OPENING MOVES

The origins of the tactics of *Blitzkrieg* and its European advocates. The rise of Hitler and the Nazis and the rearmament of Germany after 1933. The German expansion into Austria and Czechoslovakia leading up to war. Enigma and new weapons and organisations.

FALL WEISS
36-51

The German attack on Poland and use of tanks and dive bombers. The Polish air force destroyed and army trapped in pockets. Guderian comes under "friendly fire" as he advances. Junkers Ju 87 Stuka. Fighting in the Warsaw suburbs and heavy air attacks.

THE STAB IN THE BACK
58-65

Soviet Union invades Poland. Surviving Polish aircraft fly into Romania. The Army of Poznan breaks out of the Bzura pocket to Warsaw. Hitler enters Danzig. General Sikorski sets up a government in exile in Paris. Polish warships escape to Great Britain.

WEEK TWO
52-57

Poles attack in the Battle of Kutno. Polish Poznan Army smashes the 30th Infantry Division. Tanks of the 4th Panzer Division meet tough resistance in Warsaw. September 11 cohesive Polish resistance begins to collapse. Pressure on Warsaw with heavy air raids.

FALL WESERÜBUNG
66-94

Russo Finnish war of 1939-40. The German invasion of Denmark and Norway. Norwegian resistance and French and British landings. Battles of Narvik and land battle that nearly produces the first defeat for German forces in World War II. The first use of paratroops.

BLITZKRIEG

Until the autumn of 1939 wars in Europe could last for years. Leaders would attempt to find a tactical or strategic advantage – by manoeuvring to find open flanks, routes through swamps or forests or by making surprise river crossings.

In World War I the open flanks disappeared as trenches were dug that stretched from Switzerland to the North Sea. The advantage now seemed to lie with the defender. New tactics would be needed to break through these linear defences. Military theorists in Europe and America looked at deep penetration tactics using the weapons that had grown out of World War I – tanks and bombers.

At the outset of operations the enemy would be confused by a series of spoiling attacks along the length of the front while fighters dominated the skies. They would be put under pressure and have no clear idea of where the real threat lay.

Then at a few selected points the full weight of fire from tanks, artillery and bombers would be concentrated on narrow fronts. The intense weight of this bombardment shattered the defences. Reconnaissance units would probe forward and then tanks pour through the hole and into the rear areas like an expanding torrent. The enemy's defence would lose cohesion as communications links were severed, headquarters bombed, paratroops seized key points and tanks roamed unrestricted deep behind the front line. Suddenly a war between nations could be fought and won in weeks.

To describe these dramatic tactics in 1940 the journalist Eugene Hadamovsky coined a new word. He called German operations in Poland a *Blitzmarsch nach Warschau* (Lightning March to Warsaw) and from this came *Blitzkrieg* – Lightning War.

Dr Joseph Goebbels *Reichsminister für Volkserklärung und Propaganda* (Reich Minister for Public Enlightenment and Propaganda) and the Nazi propagandists seized on *Blitzkrieg* idea and revelled in its resonance.

Blitz and *Blitzkrieg* have now passed into everyday use as a synonym for intense air attacks or fast moving land battles.

This book is the first in a new series from Ian Allan Publishing telling the story of *Blitzkrieg* as practised by the German forces in World War II from Poland, through France and the Low Countries, the Balkans, Russia and North Africa. It is also the story of Panzer leaders — men of drive and vision who led from the front like Guderian, von Manstein, Kluge, Rommel and von Rundstedt.

RIGHT: In the first stage of *Blitzkrieg* bombers attack narrow front and also isolate it from communications at the rear. Small scale spoiling attacks are launched by ground forces against other parts of the front. Simultaneously tanks supported by mechanised infantry and SP artillery move up to attack the *Schwerpunkt.**

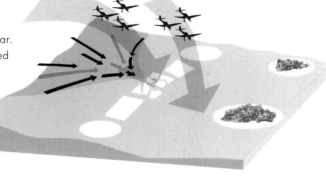

RIGHT: The front breaks at the *Schwerpunkt.* The main weight of the attack and tanks punch through the shattered defences with artillery and infantry following. Troops hold the shoulder of the breakthrough and bombers hit enemy HQs and troop concentrations.

RIGHT: Collapse sets in along the front as armoured forces fan out, isolating pockets of enemy troops and attacking positions from the rear. Bombers range deeper into the hinterland supporting the armoured thrusts.

**Schwerpunkt.* Concentrated point

THE OPENING MOVES

The hour of trial has come. When all other means have been exhausted, weapons must decide. We enter the fight knowing the justice of our cause and for a clear goal: the permanent security of the German people and German living space from foreign trespass and presumptions to power...We believe in the Führer. Forward, with God for Germany!

Order of the Day Oberkommando des Heeres September 1, 1939

At 04.45 hours on Friday September 1 1939 the still of the autumn morning on the Baltic seashore was ripped apart by the concussion of exploding shells. The air was thick with brick dust and the stench of cordite. The first salvos of World War II had crashed into the Polish fort of Westerplatte on a mile long strip of land at the mouth of the Vistula on the Danzig Corridor.

They were fired by the 13,000 ton German naval cadet training ship KMS *Schleswig-Holstein* that had opened fire at point blank range with her four 280mm (11in) guns. The

ABOVE: Towing 15cm guns SdKfz 7 half-tracks roar past the saluting base at Nuremberg on a Party Congress. The big half-track went into production in 1934 and by 1945 six companies had combined to build nearly 8,000.

big 300kg (670lb) shells from the main armament crashed into the fort. The warship was in position because she was on a "goodwill visit" to the Polish base.

Within hours the world reeled under the shock of a new and frightening way of war as it watched the violent energy of the first *Blitzkrieg* campaign of World War II begin to overwhelm Poland.

In Berlin in an early example of "media spin" the Reich Press Chief Otto Dietrich told German journalists, "The term 'war' is to be avoided at all costs in German press reports and headlines. You can describe the present situation, for example, to the effect that we are merely responding to Polish attacks".

The operation was code named *Fall Weiss* – Case White – and involved five German Armies. The speed of their advance and the ease with which they defeated the Polish armies shocked the French and British who assumed this new conflict would be an updated re-run of the trench warfare of World War I but now with modern tanks and aircraft.

Tank designs had developed, since their

LEFT: *Reichswehr* becomes *Wehrmacht* as following the introduction of conscription in March 1935 German soldiers in training leap a trench. Some are still wearing the old pattern Model 1915 steel helmet.

ABOVE: French General Charles de Gaulle one of the inter-war European tank theorists whose ideas were vindicated by the success of the German Army in its *Blitzkrieg* attacks.

together in the first all arms armoured force.

It was composed of:

A mixed battalion of armoured cars and Carden-Loyd tankettes.

A battalion of Vickers Medium tanks.

A truck mounted machine-gun battalion.

A motorised artillery regiment, plus a battery of howitzers.

A motorised engineer company.

RAF Sqdns including reconnaissance, fighter and bomber aircraft.

ABOVE: Highland soldiers man a Lewis gun covering a footbridge in the early 1930s.

introduction in World War I, and new tactics to exploit armour had been devised by British and French theoreticians like General Percy Hobart, Colonel J. F. C. Fuller and Charles de Gaulle in the 1920s and 30s. The Germans with no tanks had watched these experiments with considerable interest.

In essence a tank has three great strengths – protection, firepower and mobility. Only one tank in World War II managed to combine all three equally – the Soviet T-34. Most designs could only bring two together, some only one and a few disasters none.

British tanks in the 1920s were poor on mobility but had adequate fire power and protection. In 1927 on the Salisbury Plain training area the British Army put their tanks

TOP: A British Carden-Loyd wheel and track tankette drives down a country lane in Wiltshire.

ABOVE: Lorried infantry in their heavily camouflaged vehicle during exercises on Salisbury Plain in the 1930s.

LEFT: The shape of things to come – a Medium Tank Mk II fitted with radios.

Four years later the first full-scale exercise controlled entirely by radio was conducted on Salisbury Plain. Under Brigadier Charles Broad a force of 85 medium and 95 mixed light tanks deployed on the training area. Communications were by radio, or if there was a malfunction by flag signals.

These exercises were watched with considerable interest in Germany where the tiny defence force had no armour and was training using civilian cars like the 3/15-Ps-Dixi modified with cardboard "armour" to look like tanks. Among the officers who conducted these experiments was Heinz Guderian – a man who would have a major impact on armoured warfare.

Born in Kulm, now Chelmno in Poland, on June 17, 1888 Guderian was the son of a Prussian general. He combined in his nature the discipline and conformity of the Prussians, with an innovative mind that could find conservative officers maddening. His critics said that he was determined to prove the effectiveness of the tank arm at any price.

Educated in cadet school and commissioned into the élite Light Infantry the 10th (Hanoverian) *Jäger* Regiment in 1908, he attended the War Academy – *Kriegsakademie* – in 1913. He served as a staff officer in World War I rising through divisional, corps and finally army HQs on the Western Front.

After the war he served briefly in the volunteer armies in the Baltic states fighting to retain the territory wrested from the Russians in the Treaty of Brest Litovsk. He was selected from 32,000 wartime officers to be one of the 4,000 who would serve in the *Reichswehr*. During the 1920s and 30s, as Germany embarked on a programme of secret rearmament, he developed new armoured tactics and formed the nucleus of a mechanised force. When Hitler came to power in 1933 he recognised the potential of armoured forces and three *(Panzer)* divisions were formed.

ABOVE: Tough and professional, General Heinz Guderian the brilliant German *Blitzkrieg* theorist and practitioner. He wears the *Panzerkampfabzeichen* – the Tank Battle Badge – next to his Iron Cross First Class.

Guderian was given command of the 2nd Panzer Division and was promoted to Major-General in 1936. In 1937 he published his seminal book *Achtung-Panzer!* spelling out his ideas about armoured warfare and in 1938 was promoted to Lieutenant-General, making General by the end of the year.

He commanded the new XVI Corps during the critical days of the *Anschluss* with Austria

REICHSWEHR

Germany's military forces from 1919 – 1935 were known as the *Reichswehr*. Following the Treaty of Versailles Germany was limited to an army of 100,000 men and a navy of 15,000 while an air force was forbidden. The *Reichswehr* may have been small, but it was composed of experienced and dedicated soldiers who were keen to explore new ideas and tactics using tanks and aircraft. Disarmament of the old Imperial Army after 1918 was actually an advantage since the new force was not cluttered with weapons and equipment that was becoming obsolete, it could start with a clean slate. Even before the Nazis came to power the *Reichswehr* had established secret links with the Red Army and from 1924 tank crews were training in the USSR near the Karma River and from 1930 aircrews joined them. New secret armaments programmes were also under way using production facilities in neutral countries like Sweden and Switzerland as cover. When Hitler came to power in a speech to generals on February 3, 1933 he promised to institute a rearmament programme. In March 16, 1935 conscription was introduced and the force was renamed *die Wehrmacht*.

TOP LEFT: German infantry with a *Maschinengewehr* MG13 light machine gun.

ABOVE: New conscripts swear the *Eid* – the oath of allegiance – at a parade.

LEFT: The crew of a 750cc Schweres *Kraftrad* BMW R75 ford a shallow stream during an exercise.

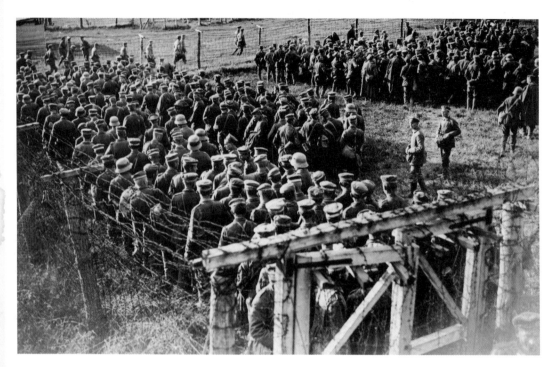

TOP: The trauma of defeat – German PoWs are collected in a temporary prison camp at the end of World War I.

ABOVE LEFT: A British screw picket on the dead soil of the Western Front. The cost in lives and exchequer of World War I beggared Germany.

ABOVE RIGHT: Dense barbed wire obstacles that stopped infantry, but could be crushed by tanks.

in 1938. Leading his tanks in a motorised dash for Vienna he was horrified to learn that at least a third had broken down. It was a useful lesson learned before fighting in Poland and later operations in more challenging theatres.

For the German public, and a disbelieving world, the pretext for the attack on Poland had been aggressive Polish border incursions. These were in reality faked incidents that included the notorious Gleiwitz Raid, the

fabricated attack on a radio station close to the German Polish border by "Polish troops". The raid at 19.30 on August 31, 1939, was undertaken by *Schutzstaffel* (SS) men dressed in mock up Polish uniforms and commanded by an SD officer, Alfred Helmut Naujocks. They beat up the radio station staff, made a brief broadcast urging Poland to attack Germany and fled leaving behind as evidence the body of one of their group. This corpse was in fact that of an inmate of a concentration camp selected as part of an operation called "Canned Goods" and shot on site by the raiders. There were other border provocations in August including an attack on the gamekeeper's house at Pitschen and the customs post at Hochinden.

For the Germans there was a feeling that they needed no justification for the attacks in the east. At the Versailles Settlement of 1919, that followed defeat in World War I, they lost their Imperial colonial empire and the

borders within Europe were redrawn. Territory went to Denmark, Poland and Belgium, while the coalfields of Alsace Lorraine, won by Prussia from France in 1871, were returned to France.

Article 231 of the Treaty of Versailles was particularly irksome to all Germans since it placed the responsibility on them for all the losses and damage of World War I. Nazis and nationalists called this the *Kriegsschuldlüge* – War Guilt Lie. They pointed out that the treaty had deprived Germany of all of its colonies in Africa – Togo, Kameroon, Southwest Africa and German East Africa passed under British control – along with the islands of the South West Pacific known as the German Pacific Territories. Germany lost its rubber and oil supplies, all its investments abroad, 15.5 per cent of its arable land, and 12 per cent of its livestock. Gone too was nearly ten per cent of its manufacturing plants, two-fifths of its coal reserves, almost two-thirds of its iron ore, and more than half of its lead. The Imperial Navy had been surrendered and scrapped and the merchant marine tonnage reduced from 5.7 million to 500,000. Feeding the anger and paranoia of post war Germany nationalist politicians asserted that the *Kriegsschuldlüge* was part of a plan to destroy the German people.

The master of this manipulation was a dark haired Austrian man of medium build who after an undistinguished youth had served with modest distinction on the Western Front in World War I. From an impoverished aspiring art student in Vienna and Munich Adolf Hitler had risen to become

SS – SCHUTZSTAFFEL

A veteran Nazi party member Heinrich Himmler formed the *Schutzstaffel,* SS or Protection Unit, in the summer of 1925 to guard Hitler. By 1929 it had a strength of 280 men. In November 1930 it was an independent force of 400 men. The major changes happened after 1933 when the SS *Verfügstruppe* (SS VT) were formed (they would be the basis of the *Waffen-SS*) the Armed SS while the rest of the SS became the *Allgemeine-*SS, the General SS. By October 1944 the *Waffen-*SS would be composed of 38 division with a strength of 910,000 men. In March 1936 the SS concentration camp guards were formed as the *Totenkopfverbände*. The *Waffen-SS* was formed in 1940 and by this time the SS Divisions *Leibstandarte-*SS Adolf Hitler, *Das Reich* and *Totenkopf* were in existence. By the close of the war the SS had become a huge organisation that ran the concentration and extermination camps, race and ethnicity and *Reich* and overseas intelligence and security. The *Sicherheitsdienst* or SD was the sinister Security Service of the SS. At the Nuremberg trial all members of the SS, with the exception of the *Waffen-SS*, were declared to be war criminals.

ABOVE: A guard of honour from the Leibstandarte-SS Adolf Hitler awaits a VIP.

the *Führer* – Leader of a new vibrant Germany that was being reconstructed from the wreckage of World War I. He was 50 when he committed his adopted country to the most destructive war of the 20th Century.

Like many men of his generation World War I had shaped his outlook at an impressionable age. As an infantryman he had fought in the Bavarian *List* Regiment that took its name from its first commanding officer Colonel von List. Its ranks contained many students and intellectuals who had volunteered. Hitler had reached the rank of Corporal and been decorated with the Iron Cross 1st and 2nd Class and the Wound Badge. In World War II, behind his back, senior officers referring to his war service nicknamed Hitler "the Bavarian Corporal".

To the veterans World War I had been a just cause that had bonded men together regardless of their status or origins. This frontline

ABOVE: Stagecraft at Nuremberg – SA chiefs Lutze and Himmler flank Hitler as they salute the tomb of the unknown warrior in the spectacular 1934 Reich Party Congress. The congress was filmed by a team directed by Leni Riefenstahl and became "Triumph of the Will".

comradeship and military prowess had been destroyed in 1918 by the *Dolchstosstheorie* – Stab in the Back Theory – which asserted that Germany had not lost the war but been destroyed from within by "Jews, traitors and Social Democrats".

For Hitler and the Nazis it was an article of faith to bring under German administration territory lost after Versailles and those *Volksdeutsche* – Ethnic Germans – trapped within it under foreign control. In East Prussia the League of Nations had established the free city of Danzig on June 28, 1919. Historically it was one of the Germanic Free

NATIONALSOZIALISTISCHE DEUTSCHE ARBEITERPARTEI

NSDAP, the National Socialist German Worker's Party, was created in April 1920 by Hitler to succeed the *Deutsche Arbeiterpartei.* Its full legal name was the *Nationalsozialistischer Deutscher Arbeiterverein* NSDAV or National Socialist German Worker's Association but in the Germany of abbreviated names it became the Nazi Party. By 1933 when Hitler came to power it was a monolithic organisation that had Hitler at the top as the *Führer* or Leader reaching down through eight layers of adminis- tration and control to the humble *Parteigenosse* or Party Comrade. Propagandists in the Union of Soviet Socialist Republics were always trou- bled by the word "Socialist" in the Nazi title and normally referred to their enemies as "Fascists".

ABOVE: The seizure of power in 1933. Hitler poses with key Party members including Göring, Himmler, Goebbels and Röhm.
BELOW LEFT: *Hitler Jugend* and *Bund Deutscher Mädel* – the Party controlled the population at all ages.
BELOW: The Volkswagen – the car that could be bought by saving five marks a week.

Ports of the Hanseatic League, but subject to the old Kingdom of Poland. At the Treaty of Versailles it was divided from Germany by the Danzig or Polish Corridor, a strip of land 15,500 sq. km (6,000 sq. miles) that gave the newly re-created state of Poland access to the Baltic Sea. In Polish eyes the corridor was originally the province of Royal (West) Prussia seized by the Hohenzollerns in 1772.

In the summer of 1939, before Italy entered the war on the side of Germany, photographs were published in *Tempo*, the Milan picture magazine, showing persecuted Germans living in the Corridor escaping to Germany. Two featured mothers with small children, one wading through marshland holding her baby, while in the other a black uniformed SS border guard assisted the pair across a barbed wire fence. The pictures were re-printed in Britain under the headline "Puerile Propaganda of the Nazi Peace-Breakers".

Before and after 1933 Nazi leaders had spoken guardedly of the *Polnische Wirtschaft*

LEBENSRAUM

For the Nazi ideologues the existence of an independent Poland was a block for *Lebensraum* – Living Space. In Hitler's geopolitics the East would provide the *Lebensraum* for the expanding Third Reich. *Lebensraum* had originally been the slogan of German expansionism in the late 19th Century as Germany worked to create a colonial empire over-seas. In 1924 following the failure of the Beer Hall putsch, an armed attempt to seize power in Munich, Hitler had dictated his political testament *Mein Kampf* while in Landsberg prison and hijacked the concept. He linked it with the racial theory of Aryan (Nordic German) superiority over Slavs and this pointed to Poland and Russia as the obvious place where a new *Lebensraum* for the new Germany could be created.

BELOW: Hitler gives the salute that with the chant *"Sieg Heil"* – Hail Victory – would be an iconic image of 1933-39.

RIGHT: Holding the *Blutfahne* – the Swastika flag carried in the Munich putsch of 1923, – Hitler "blesses" new banners at Nuremberg.

– the Polish Business – when discussing the areas of Prussia that had been ceded to Poland after 1918. In the dramatic language of nationalist propagandists these were called the "bleeding frontiers of the east".

In the west France was not seen as an area for expansion but for many ordinary non-politicised Germans the oppressive enemy

LEGION KONDOR

The Spanish Civil War had begun in July 1936 and the Germans initially deployed Ju52 transports to lift Franco's 15,000 Spanish Legion troops from Morocco to Spain. As the war expanded so did the German commitment, so by its close in 1939 the 6,000 air and tank crew and logistic personnel that had been rotated through the theatre had suffered 420 casualties killed in action. The German force known as the *Legion Kondor* – Condor Legion – wore a distinctive brown uniform. When they returned aboard a cruise liner to Germany in the summer of 1939 a parade was organised in Berlin on June 6 in which

they carried gold coloured tablets bearing the names of the Legion dead. For the *Luftwaffe* the Spanish Civil war was an excellent proving ground for Ju87 Stuka dive bombing tactics and also gave the Bf109 pilots their first experience combat. On the ground German anti-aircraft gun crews discovered that the high velocity 8.8cm Flak was a highly effective anti-tank gun – it would remain so throughout World War II.

BELOW: Ju52 transports prepare to lift Spanish troops from Morocco. Their arrival shifted the strategic balance in favour of Franco in the Civil War.

near Guadalajara. Both attacks faltered through lack of support and logistic back up and many commentators drew the conclusion that the tank should work at the pace of the infantry and not be used for deep raids.

However in the USSR preliminary work was under way to design a medium tank to replace the BT series. It would use the Christie suspension, have broad tracks, angled armour and a powerful 76mm gun. It would be called the T-34 and would change tank design forever.

The Germans grouped in a force called the *Legion Kondor* were learning valuable lessons about the limitations and effectiveness of air power. The most brutal demonstration was the attack on the undefended Basque town of Guernica on April 26, 1937. To the world it appeared a wanton act. Nine aircraft dropped 7,950 kg (7.8 tons) of bombs that were in fact intended for military targets outside the town. Casualty figures are disputed, some sources state 100 and others

that must be defeated and taught a lesson.

In July 1936 war had broken out in Spain between the Republicans who looked to Europe and the USSR for assistance and the Nationalists under General Franco who were supported by Nazi Germany and Fascist Italy. For the Germans, Italians and Soviet Union the conflict gave the opportunity to test some of their theories about armoured warfare and air power. The USSR provided about 730 Vickers-type T26s along with some early BT tanks with the distinctive American Christie suspension to support the Republicans. The Germans shipped in *PanzerKampfwagen* (PzKpfw) I tanks and the Italians the little Fiat Ansaldo C33 to back up the Nationalists.

On October 29, 1936 the Russian General Pavlov working with the Republicans attempted a deep armoured raid with 50 tanks at Esquivas and again in March 1937

TOP LEFT: Massed drummers and trumpeters of the Hitler Jugend at Nuremberg.

ABOVE: The distinctive lines of the M1915 with the *Wehrmachtadler* eagle and Swastika decal that was phased out on all helmets from 1940.

ABOVE: Tea with the *Führer*. British Prime Minister Neville Chamberlain at one of several meetings he held as he attempted to influence Hitler. On the right is Sir Nevile Henderson the British Ambassador. Though Chamberlain was accused of appeasement he launched a rearmament programme after 1938.

1,600 were killed, but what was not disputed was the destruction of 71% of the town. With the benefit of hindsight Guernica showed that tactical and later strategic bombing was a double-edged weapon, sometimes failing to hit the target and often producing adverse propaganda.

Hitler had chosen August 26, 1939 as the date for the attack on Poland, however on the day he ordered a postponement. It was not the first example of the behaviour that would dog his conduct of operations throughout the war – mixing of high-risk options and indecision. Some units only received the cancellation orders a mere hour or two before H Hour. It actually failed to reach one small group tasked with the capture of a Polish railway station and tunnel in the southwest. They went into action, opened fire and caused casualties and so fired the first shots of World War II. A truce was agreed the next day and they returned to Germany. The Poles were not alerted by this action because in the recent months there had been numerous incidents on the border.

Then six days later the first salvos crashed into the fort at Westerplatte, held only by a company of Polish soldiers, and now the war was on in earnest. Following the bombardment the tiny garrison repelled a landing by

German naval forces, inflicted casualties and held out until September 7.

As with so many of Hitler's moves in World War II the attack was a gamble. The German Army had completed autumn manoeuvres and so was still in the field. However the Führer and the staff of the OKW, *Oberkommando des Wehrmacht* (High Command of the Armed Forces) knew that two thirds of the German strength on land and in the air would have to be committed to the attack. It was vital that Poland should be defeated before France and Great Britain had time to declare war, mobilise and attack in the west.

For France and Great Britain the attack on Poland was the final fatal move. Committed to defending Poland in a treaty signed on August 23, 1939, Great Britain declared war on Nazi Germany at 11.00 on September 3, 1939 and France followed at 17.00. In Britain the public had tuned their radios into the Home Service and heard the Prime Minister Neville Chamberlain explain quietly that the British government had requested that Germany should withdraw her troops from Poland.

He ended the broadcast with the resigned

BELOW: Hitler ascends to the podium past massed SA banners at a rally at Bückeberg in 1934. These vast stage-managed events helped to establish Hitler's position as *Führer* – leader – and his popularity with ordinary Germans.

PzKpfw I Ausf B

Built by Daimler-Benz, Henschel, Krupp, MAN and Wegmann before and during the war the *Panzerkampfwagen* (PzKpfw) I was an interim vehicle intended for training. In different marks it would however serve in Poland, France and even the opening moves of the campaign in the USSR. The Ausf B entered service in 1935.

SPECIFICATIONS

Armament:	2 x 7.92mm (0.31in) MG (2,250 rounds)
Armour:	13mm (0.51in)
Crew:	2
Weight:	5,800kg (5.71tons)
Hull length:	4.42m (14ft 6in)
Width:	2.06m (6ft 9in)
Height:	1.72m (5ft 8in)
Engine:	Maybach NL38TR 6-cylinder, petrol, 100bhp at 3,000rpm.
Road speed:	40km/h (25mph)
Range:	170km (105miles)

ABOVE: The November 8 Parade in Munich in which the names of the men killed in the *Putsch* were read out. Nazi ideologists created a myth of the death and rebirth of the Party.

RIGHT: Hitler returns to Austria as he begins his territorial expansion in 1938 following the *Anschluss*.

words "No reply has been received from the German government and consequently a state of war now exists between Great Britain and Germany".

On the evening of that day the German submarine U-30 sank the British liner SS *Athenia*. It was an error, but American passengers were among the dead.

The indicators of Hitler's voracious territorial ambitions and the inevitability of war had culminated in the Munich Agreement signed in September 29 – 30, 1938 between Germany, Italy, France and Britain.

The first was on March 7, 1936 when in an operation code named Winter Exercise Hitler ordered about one division of German troops to enter the Rhineland, a strip of land about 60 km long to the west of the River Rhine. It had been demilitarised since 1918 as part of the Treaty of Versailles, a treaty ratified at the Locarno Pact. The area included the cities of Cologne, Düsseldorf and Bonn and all the territory to the west

The *Rheinlandbesetzung* – Rhineland Reoccupation – was Hitler's first foreign policy coup. His generals were concerned that the German army was not strong enough to defeat a concerted attack by the French –

it never happened and Hitler scored a victory over his military detractors as well as the West.

Austria, a neighbour to the south that had been created out of the old Austro- Hungarian Hapsburg Empire, was entirely German speaking, and significantly included the Führer's birthplace. Its population was obviously *Volksdeutsche* and thus it was natural that they should be united with Germany through the Union or *Anschluss*. The Austrian Nazis fronted by Artur Seyss-Inquart had pressed for union with Germany and the Austrian Legion, the military arm of the Austrian Nazis, had waged a guerrilla war

The Enigma was a highly sophisticated mechanical encryption system that had a keyboard and looked superficially like a typewriter. The German engineer Arthur Scherbius developed it in 1923 from a design by a Dutchman H.A. Koch. The German Army and Navy saw its potential and bought it in 1929. The Germans believed that it would make the transmission of radio messages faster and completely secure. In its simplest form for every letter it sent there were hundreds of millions of possible solutions. However the Germans forgot how few letters there are in the alphabet; that no letter could stand for itself; and that the machine had no number keys so that figures had to be spelled out. The Poles began reading some signals in 1932, the French intelligence services in 1938 and the British in February 1940. For the British the secrecy of the project was at such a high level that they classified it as "Ultra Secret" and so it became ULTRA.

ABOVE: Rhinelanders greet German troops as they march into the demilitarised zone in the *Rheinlandbesetzung* of March 1936. Hitler's generals were fearful that the French would attack following this breach of the Armistice agreements, but the French did nothing.

against the government in Vienna.

On March 12, 1938 in an operation code named Otto, German troops entered Austria on the "invitation" of the Chancellor Kurt Schuschnigg. The code name had been selected because Otto of Hapsburg, the young pretender to the throne, was alive and living in exile in Belgium and moves to prevent his

restoration were part of the cover story for armed intervention. The German troops had been called in to "protect" Austria.

On March 15 in front of huge crowds at Vienna's Heldenplatz Hitler announced amid thunderous jubilation "the entry of my home-land into the German Reich".

The centuries old name of Österreich was abolished and replaced with the archaic Ostmark – the Eastern Marches – and Austria was absorbed into a country that was fast becoming Greater Germany.

In September that year the Munich Agreement ceded the German speaking Sudetenland of western Czechoslovakia to Germany. In August 1938 Hitler had mobilised his army and threatened to attack the Czechs. The British and French Prime Ministers Chamberlain and Daladier had a series of meetings in which they were pres-surised by Hitler and in turn pressed the Czechs. At Munich a modified version of Hitler's demands was deemed acceptable to the Anglo French leaders. This appeasement allowed Hitler to further dominate his generals, who believed that France and Britain would call the Führer's bluff and go to war. The French and British leaders were gleefully portrayed by Nazi propaganda as weak and vacillating.

In March 1939 the Germans took over the whole of Czechoslovakia and were able to add the excellent indigenous Skoda LT-35 and Ceskomoravska Kolben Danek (CDK) LT-38 tanks to their inventory of armoured vehicles. The Czechs had exported tanks to Sweden, Hungary, Yugoslavia, Latvia and even Afghanistan and Peru. The *Wehrmacht* received approximately 300 LT-35s and with the designation PzKpfw 35(t) they were formed into a panzer division. Two more divisions were made up from the excellent LT-38 now designated PzKpfw 38(t).

The Munich Agreement was seen as the

THE POLISH ARMY SEPTEMBER 1, 1939

From the north the Polish armies were:

Narew Army
General Mlot-Fijalkowski
18th and 33rd Infantry Divisions (Inf Divs)
"Suwalki" and "Podlaska" Cavalry Brigades
(Cav Bdes).

Wyskow Group
General Skarczinski,
1st, 35th and 41st Inf Divs
(the 5th and 44th Inf Divs were moving up to
Kutno and the 22nd and 38th to Przemysl).

Modlin Army
General Przedrzymirski,
8th and 20th Inf Divs,
"Mazow" and "Nowogrod" Cav Bdes.

Pomorze (Pomeranian) Army
General Bortnowski
4th, 9th, 15th, 16th, 27th Inf Divs,
"Pomerania" Cav Bde.

Poznan Army
General Tadeusz Kutrzeba
14th, 17th, 25th and 26th Inf Divs,
"Great Poland" and "Podolia" Cav Bdes.

Lodz Army
General Juliusz Rómmel
2nd, 10th, 28th and 30th Inf Divs,
"Border" and "Wolhynia" Cav Bdes.

Cracow Army
General Antoni Szylling
6th, 7th, 212st, 23rd, 45th and 55th Inf
Divs,
"Krakow" Cav Bde.

Carpathian Army
General Kazimierz Fabrycy
11th, 24th and 38th Inf Divs,
2nd and 3rd Mountain Bdes.

Reserves included the:
Prusy (Prussian) Army
General Dab-Biernacki
3rd, 12th, 13th, 19th, 29th
and 36th Inf Divs,
"Vilna" Cav Bde.

Pyskor Group
39th Inf Div
"Warsaw" Armoured Bde.

low point of the policy of Appeasement, but it was also an awakening in the West to the threat posed by Nazi Germany. It bought time for Britain and France who now began to accelerate re-armament and in conjunction with Poland work began on breaking the German Enigma code machines.

This decryption operation was still in its infancy in the autumn 1939 and could not save Poland. However Poland's collapse was accelerated by the surprise invasion of eastern Poland by the Red Army on September 17.

A major tenet of National Socialism had been intense hostility towards Communism. In his speeches in the 1930s Hitler had rolled anti-Semitism and hatred of "Bolshevism" into ranting outbursts that had enraptured his audiences. On April 7, 1939 Germany, Italy, Spain and Japan had signed the Anti-

LEFT: A heavy anti-aircraft gun crew during a training exercise. The ability of Germany to defend itself against air attack with guns and fighters was a popular and potent myth.

RIGHT: Using their 70cm *Entfernungsmesser* range finders a 2cm Flak crew give range corrections on the approaching aircraft. The gunners would adjust their sights until they could correct their aim by observing the tracer.

LEFT: The superb 8.8cm Flak that would prove as effective as an anti-tank gun as it was an AA gun. During the war new carriages would be developed to give it a lower silhouette.

THE POLISH AIR FORCE IN 1939

The outnumbered *Lotnictwo Wojskowe* – Polish Air Force – had some excellent aircraft like the PZL-P11c and P.37B that put up a brief but doomed resistance to the fighters of the *Luftwaffe*. Some pilots later escaped to join the RAF.

PZL-P11c

In the mid 1930s the Polish National Aero Factory (PZL) produced a new monoplane fighter, the PZL P11, that became the object of international interest and respect. However by 1939 the PZL P11c that equipped 12 of the Lotnictwo Wojskowe fighter squadrons were outclassed by the Messerschmitt Bf109. The PZL P11c has the distinction of being the first fighter in World War II to shoot down a Luftwaffe aircraft, a Ju87 dive bomber. By the close of the campaign PZL P11 fighters had downed 125 enemy aircraft. The only operational model of the intended successor, the PZL P50, was shot down by Polish AA fire since its modern silhouette was confused with that of a German aircraft.

SPECIFICATIONS
Type: Interceptor fighter
Crew: 1
Power Plant: One 645hp (Skoda built) Bristol
               Mercury VIS.2
Performance: Maximum speed at 5,500m
               (18,050ft) 390km/h (242mph)
Normal range: 700km (435 miles)
Weights: Empty 1,147kg (2,529lb)
               Maximum 1,800kg (3,968lb)
Dimensions: Wing span 10.72m (35ft 2 in)
Length: 7.55m (24ft 9in)
Height: 2.85m (9ft 4in)
Armament: Two 7.7mm (0.303in) KM Wz 33
               machine guns and 50kg
               (110lb) underwing bomb load.

MODEL P.37B LOS B (ELK)

The pride of the *Lotnictwo Wojskowe*, the P.37B Los was a modern twin engined bomber that first flew in mid 1938. By 1939 some 95 had been built and 40 were in front line service. Flying on reconnaissance and ground attack missions 25 were lost to enemy action. Surviving aircraft flew to Romania and were later used by the Romanians in the attack on the USSR in 1941. The remarkable bomber remained in service after World War II until the mid 1950s operating as target tug for fighter training.

SPECIFICATIONS
Type: Twin engined medium bomber
Crew: 4
Power Plant: Two 918hp (PZL built) Bristol Pegasus
Performance: Maximum speed at 3,400m (11,150ft)
               445km/h (277mph)
Maximum range: 4,500km (2,796miles)
Weights: Empty 4,280kg (9,436lb)
               Maximum 8,900kg (16,620lb)
Dimensions: Wing span 17.93m (58ft 10in)
Length: 12.92m (42ft 4in)
Height: 5.08m (16ft 8in)
Armament: One 7.7mm (0.303in) KM Wz 37
               machine gun in nose, dorsal and ventral
               positions and 2,580kg (5,688lb)
               bomb load

ABOVE: French soldiers in working dress sit on the rudder of an He111 downed during the 1939 – 40 Phoney War.

RIGHT: A local victory, the bullet scarred cockpit of an He111 bomber shot down by French fighters in 1939.

Comintern Pact linking these countries in opposition to Communism. It caused shock and surprise therefore to Communists, Nazis and conservative Germans alike when on August 20, 1939 Hitler telegrammed Stalin to urge an agreement because of the "worsening situation in Poland".

On August 23, 1939 the Russo-German Pact was signed in Moscow by the German Foreign Minister Joachim von Ribbentrop and Soviet Foreign Minister Vyacheslav Molotov. Hitler in a piece of brutal pragmatism had ensured that the USSR would not

intervene to support the Poles and paved the way for the German invasion in September that year and allowed the USSR to extend its western borders by seizing areas of Poland.

With the political ground prepared the Germans launched a two pronged attack on Poland. Army Group North under General Fedor von Bock consisting of the 3rd Army under General Georg von Küchler in East Prussia punched south and 4th Army under General Hans von Kluge with the XIX Panzer Corps commanded by General Guderian drove east from Prussia. To the south the 8th Army commanded by General Johannes Blaskowitz drove towards Lodz.

Army Group South under General Gerd von Rundstedt consisting of the 10th Army under General Walter von Reichenau and the XVI Panzer Corps under General Erich Hoepner drove north towards Warsaw. In Slovakia the 14th Army under General Wilhelm von List

ABOVE: Mail call for French troops in 1939. Poor leadership and low morale would undermine the army in the bitter winter of 1939 – 40

pushed north into the industrial areas around Cracow.

Their mission was to carry out a pincer movement to surround and destroy the bulk of Polish forces west of the Vistula-Narev line.

The Polish ground forces ranged opposite them, commanded by Marshal Edward Rydz-Smigly, were grouped to face a threat from the west.

The Polish armies positioned close to the border in linear defences under a scheme designated Plan Z or "West" could not have been worse sited to withstand a *Blitzkrieg* attack. The Polish planners knew that they could not withstand an all out German attack and hoped that French and British forces in the West would attack Germany and so draw

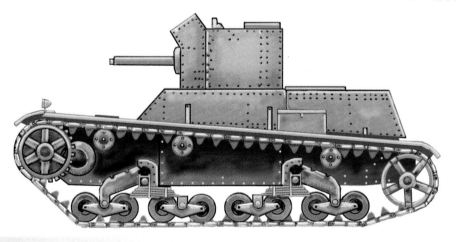

7 TP

The Polish development of the British Vickers Six-Ton tank the 7 TP was originally built with twin central turrets, two twin bogies each side, front sprocket, rear idler. The 7TP-2 produced in 1937 was fitted with a turret with a Swedish Bofors 37mm (1.45in) anti-tank gun. About 170 had been built and most were lost in the fighting in 1939. A final development, the 7TP-3 with a new turret, thicker amour, new engine and wider tracks went into production in 1939 but few saw action.

SPECIFICATIONS

Armament:	2 x 7.92mm (0.31in) MG
Armour:	17mm (0.66in)
Crew:	3
Weight:	9,550kg (9.4tons)
Hull length:	4.60m (15ft 1in)
Width:	2.16m (7ft 1in)
Height:	2.13m (7ft)
Engine:	Saurer diesel, 6-cylinder, 110hp
Road speed:	32km/h (20mph)
Range:	160km (100miles)

TK3

Developed in 1931 the TK-3 was based on open topped "tankette" vehicles copied from the British Carden-Loyd design. The TK-3 had improved double bogie suspension with a supporting girder and a fully enclosed crew compartment. About 390 had been built and in 1938 a few were upgunned with a 20mm (0.78in) gun and given thicker armour.

SPECIFICATIONS

Armament:	1 x 9.92mm (0.31in) MG or 20mm (0.78in) gun
Armour:	8mm (0.31in)
Crew:	2
Weight:	2,500kg (2.46tons)
Hull length:	2.65m (8ft 6in)
Width:	1.55m (5ft 10in)
Height:	1.35m (4ft 4in)
Engine:	Ford A, 4-cylinder, petrol, 40bhp at 2,300rpm
Road speed:	45km/h (28mph)
Range:	200km (125miles)

off some of the pressure. The flat wheat fields of Poland offered few natural obstacles on which to base a defence, but rivers like the Bzura, Narev, Bug and the Vistula were considerable barriers.

When fully mobilised the Polish Army would have had a strength of 3,600,000 men. The Poles had a tiny armoured force divided into nine companies of light tanks and 29 companies of light scout cars.

In 1928 the Poles had bought Carden-Loyd light tanks and in 1932 Vickers tanks from Britain. These two vehicles formed the basis for locally built TK light tanks. The first were the TK-1 and TK-2 open topped two man vehicles armed with a machine gun, they were followed by the TK-3 reconnaissance vehicle. The 7 TP light tank based on the Vickers Six-Ton was initially armed with two machine guns, but the 7TP-2, of which about 170 were built, mounted a Swedish Bofors 37mm anti-tank gun with a coaxial 7.92mm

machine gun. The 7TP-3 had thicker armour, stronger suspension and wider tracks. It went into production in 1939 but few reached front line formations.

In the West on September 7 the French forces caused some consternation in the OKW when they began a slow advance into the Saarland, but they did not attack the *Westwall*, the line of fortifications close to the German border.

Given the grand name "Operation Saar" it was directed by General Gaston Prételat. Though he had 31 divisions available for the operation, including 14 first line units, he only used nine. General Edouard Réquin's 4th Army managed to capture 12km (7 miles) of German territory while General Condé's 3rd

BELOW: British troops help bring in the harvest in France in the autumn of 1939. Though not military training, activity like this helped to keep men busy and maintain morale.

LEFT: A German NCO and soldier captured by French troops in 1939, in less than a year the roles would be reversed.

BELOW: French soldiers on the Maginot Line with a grenade thrower and Chatellerault M1924/29 LMG.

THE RUSSO GERMAN PACT 1939

The pact ensured that :

1) Neither party would attack the other.

2) Should one of them become the object of belligerent action by a third power the other party would in no manner lend its support to this third power.

3) Neither Germany nor Russia would join any grouping of Powers whatsoever aimed directly or indirectly at the other party.

A secret protocol identified spheres of interest in Poland and the Baltic;
the USSR had claims on Finland, Estonia, Latvia and Lithuania with the northern border of Lithuania as a diving line.
In Poland Soviet influence would reach as far as the line of the rivers Narev, Vistula and San.

Army pinched out the heavily wooded Warndt Forest salient. The Germans had already evacuated the area and during the operation the French suffered 27 killed, 22 wounded with 28 missing. The *L'Armée de l'Air* under General Joseph Vuillemin lost nine fighters and 18 reconnaissance aircraft.

On the morning of September 12, the French Havas News Agency reported a complacent French Army communiqué: "Last night passed quietly on the whole of the Western Front".

By October 4 the French had withdrawn their forces from the Saarland and were safe back behind the defences of the Maginot Line to sit out the winter in comfort.

FALL WEISS

Ade Polenland,

Ade weites Land,

Heim geht jetzt die Fahrt.

Wollen heimwärts ziehn,

Wo die Kirschen blühn,

Manches Mädel auf uns harrt.

Ade Polenland – "Goodbye Poland" – German marching song.

In the east in great curving thrusts the attacking German tanks and mechanised infantry supported by dive-bombers cut off the Polish armies. The Germans were enjoying "Führer's weather" – a dry sunny autumn, perfect for flying and ideal for trucks and armoured vehicles. The Poles prayed for cloud and rain – it would come a few days after their last units had surrendered.

The *Luftwaffe* had more than 3,600 operational aircraft and deployed 1,500 for the attack on Poland. Of these 897 were bombers and 426 fighters with additional reconnaissance and transport aircraft. Opposite them the Polish

ABOVE: Hitler meets the Polish Foreign Minister Colonel Jozef Beck in the last days of peace.

ABOVE: An He111 seen from the glazed cockpit of another bomber in the formation.

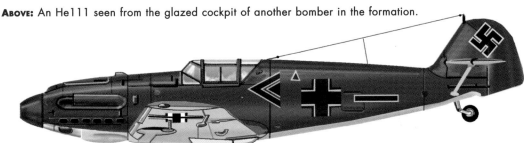

MESSERSCHMITT BF109D-1

By the time war broke out in 1939 the Bf109D-1 was being replaced by the superior E-1 variant. However it participated in the Polish campaign. It was also used as an interim night-fighter in the defence of northern Germany until the Spring of 1940. The Bf109D-1 was not popular because its DB 600A engine was not reliable. The fighters were built at Arada, Erla, Focke-Wulf and Fieseler plants with over 30,500 of all marks being built in Germany.

SPECIFICATIONS

Type:	Single engined fighter
Crew:	1
Power Plant:	One 984hp Daimler-Benz DB 600Aa3
Performance:	Maximum speed at sea level 480km/h (298mph)
Maximum range:	600km (348miles)
Weights:	Empty 1,800kg (3,964lb)
	Maximum 2,420kg (5,335lb)
Dimensions:	Wing span 9.87m (32ft 4in)
Length:	8.6m (28ft 2in)
Height:	2.56m (8ft 4in)
Armament:	One 20mm MG FF cannon in propeller hub, two 7.92mm (0.31in) MG 17 in upper cowling.

ABOVE: Messerschmitt Bf109D fighters in an airfield in Germany. These were the aircraft that won the *Luftwaffe* air superiority over Poland and paved the way for the success of *Blitzkrieg*.

Air Force – *Lotnictwo Wojskowe* – commanded by Maj General J. Zajac had approximately 1,900 aircraft and deployed 400, of these 154 were bombers, 159 fighters and the rest reconnaissance or liaison aircraft. The German aircraft were more modern and technically superior. In the first days, despite heroic fighting much of the *Lotnictwo Wojskowe* had ceased to exist and the German bombers and ground attack aircraft were free to concentrate on destroying communications like bridges and

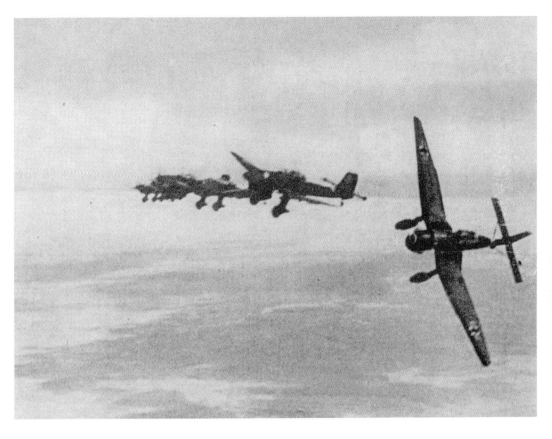

ABOVE: Stukas peel off to attack. The howl of the diving aircraft as well as their accuracy made them a very effective psychological weapon.

LEFT: A Junkers Flugzeug und Motorwerke advertisement celebrates the Ju87 Stuka dive bomber.

railways as well as more immediate military targets like headquarters and airfields.

The commanders of the Lotnictwo Wojskowe had anticipated a German air attack and though their airfields were destroyed, the planes on the ground were non-fliers grounded with mechanical problems. Airworthy planes had been dispersed to emergency strips and put up a brief and brave defence.

Among the more colourful *Luftwaffe* dive bomber experts whose aircraft attacked the Polish airfields and bridges was Wolfram Freiherr von Richthofen. He was a cousin of Manfred von Richthofen, the World War I fighter ace known as the "Red Baron" and commander of the squadron known as the "Flying Circus". In 1936 Wolfram had served as Chief of Staff to General Hugo Sperrle and *Generalmajor* Helmuth Volkmann, the commanders of the *Legion Kondor* in Spain. In 1938 as an *Oberst* von Richthofen was its final commander. In Poland he commanded the *Fliegerkorps* VIII, three squadrons of Ju87 Stukas that became "flying artillery" providing very efficient close support for the Panzers.

The problem of correct aircraft recognition

LEFT: Concealed in scrub a German soldier in a reconnaissance patrol observes a Polish position through his field glasses. Constructed from aluminium alloy the field glasses were light, easy to use and issued widely in the German Army.

PzKpfw II Ausf A, B, C

Built by Alkett, Daimler-Benz, FAMO, Henschel, MAN, MIAG and Wegmann the Panzer II entered service in 1937.

A fast reconnaissance vehicle, it had a 20mm cannon. The Ausf A was the full production model of the tank and was considerably different from the two pre-production versions.

SPECIFICATIONS

Armament:	1 x 20mm (0.78in) (180 rounds), 1 x 7.92mm (0.31in) MG (2,250 rounds)
Armour:	16mm (0.62in)
Crew:	3
Weight:	8,900kg (8.75tons)
Hull length:	4.81m (15ft 9in)
Height:	1.99m (6ft 6in)
Engine:	Maybach HL62TR, 6-cylinder petrol, 140bhp at 2,600rpm
Road speed:	40km/h (25mph)
Range:	200km (125miles)

Legend:
- Soviet invasion Sept 17
- Polish armies
- German attacks
- Polish pockets

LITHUANIA

Memel
Dvina
Polotzk
Kaunas
Vilna
Minsk

Polwysep Hel
Konigsberg
Gdynia Danzig

GERMANY

Suwalki
Niemen

Stettin
Chelmno
Bialystok

Oder
Torun
Vistula
Modlin

Frankfurt
Gniezno
WARSAW
Brest-Litovsk

Poznan
Kutno

Glogau
Lodz
Gora Kalwaria

Breslau
Wielun
Piotrkow
Deblin

POLAND

Oppeln
Tomaszow

Ostrava
Krakow
L'Vov

GERMANY
Dniestr

SLOVAKIA

RUMANIA

Bratislava

HUNGARY

USSR

ABOVE: Surrounded on three sides by German armies Poland was easy meat for the Panzer Divisions that split the Polish forces up into pockets and then destroyed them.

RIGHT: Mounted German troops advance through Poland. Though the Panzers were the cutting edge many soldiers marched or rode on horseback.

LEFT: The twisted remains of a major road and rail link, either bombed by the *Luftwaffe* or demolished by Polish Army engineers. The speed of the German advance nullified many of the Polish attempts to create obstacles and barriers by demolitions.

RIGHT: General Guderian watches in his SdKfz 251 half track command vehicle as a signal is decoded. The Enigma encryption machine has been cropped out of the bottom of the picture by the wartime German censor.

BELOW RIGHT: With vestigial camouflage against a non-existent air threat German gunners prepare a 15cm sFH 18 medium howitzer for a fire mission.

that would bedevil all combatants in World War II appeared in the campaign in Poland. Colonel von Mellenthin, the Intelligence Officer with III Corps, recalled:

"A low flying aircraft circled over Corps battle headquarters and everyone let fly with whatever he could grab. An air-liaison officer ran out trying to stop the fusillade and shouting to the excited soldiery that this was a German command plane – one of the good old Fieseler Störche. Soon afterwards the aircraft landed and out stepped the *Luftwaffe* general responsible for our close air support. He failed to appreciate the joke".

Offshore in the Baltic the *Kriegsmarine* – the German Navy – had the modern battle cruisers KMS *Scharnhorst* and *Gneisenau*, three "pocket battleship" light battle cruisers, two heavy cruisers, six light cruisers, 22 destroyers and 43 U-boats. There were two obsolete pre-Dreadnought battleships, the *Schlesien* and the *Schleswig-Holstein*, the latter had opened the fighting. The Polish Navy under Rear Admiral Jozef Swirski had only three modern destroyers and five modern submarines as well as 23 aircraft and a small number of coastal craft.

The six Panzer and four Light Divisions that formed the cutting edge of the ground attack on Poland were still only equipped with PzKpfw I and PzKpfw II light tanks and ex-Czech PzKpfw 38(t) and 35(t) tanks. The

PzKpfw I was essentially a training vehicle armed only with two MG 34 machine guns. The *Panzer Lehr* Demonstration Battalion, a training battalion, had been added to Guderian's XIX Corps at his request and deployed its PzKpfw III and PzKpfw IV tanks. The former were armed with a short barrelled 3.7cm gun and the latter with a 7.5cm. Guderian had also requested that the Reconnaissance Demonstration Battalion be attached to his Corps. For Guderian, the passionate armour theorist, Poland was a unique opportunity to test new equipment in action. When later in the campaign he was visited by Hitler he took the opportunity to press for the adoption of the PzKpfw III and IV and that they should have thicker armour and more powerful guns.

In fact the Polish armoured opposition and anti-tank defences represented no real threat to the German forces who were however able to test techniques of command and control. At one end this was amply demonstrated by

ABOVE: The gunner on an MG34 observes through the gun's optical sight.

BELOW: *A Flammenwerfer* 35 flamethrower crew advance through their smoking handiwork.

PzKpfw III Ausf C

Built initially by Daimler-Benz in the late 1930s the PzKpfw III was not available in large numbers at the time of the invasion of Poland. Some 17 Ausf C and 30 Ausf D were deployed as well as some Ausf E. The Ausf C had a brief operational career being scrapped after the campaign in Poland. When later marks of the tank were armed with a more powerful 5cm L/42 gun the tank became a formidable opponent in North Africa. However like the PzKpfw IV it was no match for the T-34 and German engineers were forced to develop new designs like the Tiger and Panther.

SPECIFICATIONS

Armament:	1 x 37mm (1.45in), 3 x 7.92mm (0.31in) MG ds
Armour:	1 x 37mm (1.45in),
Crew:	3
Weight:	16,000kg (15.75tons)
Hull length:	5.85m (19ft 2in)
Hull width: `	2.82m (9ft 3in)
Height:	2.42m (7ft 11in)
Engine:	Maybach HL108TR, V-12 petrol, 250bhp at 3,000rpm 140bhp at 2,600rpm
Road speed:	40km/h (25mph)
Range:	165km (100miles)

a Panzer Regiment commanded by *Oberst* Wilhelm Ritter von Thoma – a veteran of armoured operations in Spain. It outflanked a Polish position at the Jublenka Pass by making a 80.5km (50 mile) night march through densely wooded hill country and so achieved complete surprise.

On the larger scale Guderian handled his XIX Corps, composed of two Panzer and two Motorised Divisions, as single entity leading it from the front in an SdKfz 251/6 half track armoured command vehicle.

The SdKfz215/6 *mittler Kommando Panzerwagen* had a distinctive frame antenna

for the onboard radios linked to their Enigma encryption equipment. His driver nearly ended the career of this illustrious commander when on the first day as they advanced through morning mist they came under unexpected artillery fire. Guderian was such an enthusiastic exponent of forward command that his own gunners had taken his vehicle to be Polish.

Guderian ordered his driver to turn round and move away, however he panicked and drove the half track at full speed into a ditch, bending the front axle and rendering the vehicle immobile. "This" remarked Guderian "marked the end of my first drive".

The right flank of the Pomorze Army under Brigadier General Boltuc was beaten after a two-day battle along the River Ursa and Lake Melno and pushed south. A thrust by the XIX Panzer Corps broke the Polish defence on the western bank of the Vistula along the Brahe on the first day of fighting. The German tanks reached the Vistula and around the southern Tuchel Heath cut off two Polish infantry divisions and a cavalry brigade that were trying

BELOW: An MG34 crew prepare to give covering fire over an improvised Polish road block. The MG34 was the first General Purpose Machine Gun that could be used in the light or medium medium role and fired by one man.

RIGHT: A grenadier pitches a stick grenade into a Polish position. The *Stielhandgranate* 24 was easy to operate, the friction pull cord was in the hollow handle covered by a screw cap and gave a delay of 4 to 5 seconds.

to withdraw through the Corridor to Chelmno and Grudziadz. The Danzig Corridor was no more, the Pomorze Army had lost 50 per cent of its strength and was forced back to Torun and Bydgoszcz.

The Poznan Army under General Kutrzeba had only limited contacts in the first few days of the campaign. The Lodz Army however fought for two days against the combined forces of the German 8th and 14th Armies.

On Saturday September 2 the situation of

10TH BRYGADA KAWALERII

In 1937 the motorised 10th Brygada Kawalerii – Motorised Cavalry Brigade – under General Maczek was formed and became the first Polish armoured force. It was composed of two motorised cavalry regiments, one division (Div) of armoured cars, an anti-tank gun Div, a company (Coy) of Vickers 6 ton tanks, a TKS reconnaissance tank Coy, a motorised artillery (75mm and 100mm guns) Div, an AA gun battery, an engineer platoon (Ptn), a signals Ptn, a traffic control Ptn and a transport Coy. On August 31, 1939 it had a strength of 1,515 officers, 8,949 NCOs and 18,020 men. Tragically at the outset of World War II the force that was part of the Army of Cracow was parcelled out into 15 independent companies and attached to infantry and cavalry formations and never used as a formed armoured brigade against the Germans. Maczek managed to evade capture at the end of the campaign and reach France where he commanded an armoured brigade.

JUNKERS JU87 B-1

The Ju87, universally known as the Stuka from the German acronym for *Sturzkampfflugzeug* – diving warplane – developed a reputation as an awesome instrument of war during the Polish campaign. The scream of the diving aircraft was terrifying to men attacked on the ground. Some aircraft were fitted with sirens called *Jericho-Trompeten* – the Trumpets of Jericho – fitted to the spatted undercarriage to enhance the psychological shock. It was superb in a close support role where AA defence was negligible and where hostile fighters were not present. At the outbreak of war the Luftwaffe had 336 Ju87B-1s on its strength.

SPECIFICATIONS

Type:	Single engined dive-bomber
Crew:	2
Power Plant:	One Jumo 1,200hp Junkers Jumo 211Da
Performance:	Maximum speed at 4,090m (13,410ft) 383km/h (238mph)
Weights:	Empty 2,420kg (5,335lb) Maximum 2,710kg (5,980lb)
Dimensions:	Wing span 13.8m (45ft 3in)
Length:	8.6m (28ft 2in)
Height:	4.01m (13ft 2in)
Armament:	Two fixed forward firing 7.92mm (0.31in) MG 17 in wings, one flexible MG15 on rear cockpit, max bomb load 500kg (1,102lb)

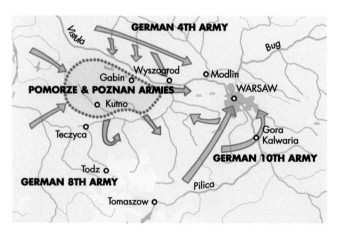

LEFT: The Battle of Bzura
The Polish breakout by the Pomorze and Poznan Armies towards Warsaw through the German 8th and 4th Armies. Stuka attacks hit the Bzura bridges.

RIGHT: A German MG34 crew dash past a burned down building. The gun fired from 50 round belts at 800 to 900 rounds a minute.

the Cracow Army was critical and the threat from the north and south forced General Szylling to order a withdrawal along the Vistula behind the Rivers Dunajec and Nida. With Polish forces withdrawing a gap developed in the central sector between Czestochowa, Pietrkow, Kielce and Sandomierz.

By Saturday evening after Germans had encircled the left flank of the Lodz Army the Polish forces were forced to withdraw from their positions on along the Rivers Warta and Widawaka. They were under intense pressure from the XV and XVI Panzer Corps that had pushed into the gap between the Lodz and Cracow Armies and smashed the Polish 7th Infantry Division under Brigadier General Gasiorowski.

This allowed the 10th Army to push towards Pietrkow and Kielce and threaten to encircle the Cracow Army from the north. At this point the Cracow Army started receiving reports that German forces had appeared in the Beskid Mountains on their left flank. This was the 17th and 22nd Corps part of the 14th Army.

Despite the critical situation of his armies Marshal Rydz-Smigly still believed that the Polish armies could pull back to defensive positions on river lines and hold the assaults.

On Sunday September 3 General Kasprzycki was ordered to prepare Warsaw for defence. To the north of the city troops commanded by General Przedrzymirski-Krukowiecki that had held positions at Mlawa against attacks by the 1st Corps was forced to withdraw during the night of September 3 – 4 to avoid encirclement.

On Monday General Piskor took command of the Polish forces along the central Vistula

and formed them into the Army of Lublin. To block Polish forces withdrawing behind the Vistula the Army Group South ordered the 14th Army to drive for the River San. Meanwhile the right flank of the 10th Army was to block the withdrawal of Polish troops from the area of Kielce-Radom, while its left flank was to smash forces in the Pietrkow-Tomaszow Maz area and advance on Warsaw to cut off the withdrawal of the enemy from Lodz and Poznan. *Luftwaffe* dive bombers flying continuous sorties had pulverised the Modlin Army and it crossed the Vistula leaving Warsaw unprotected from the north.

The German 3rd Army had pushed from Ciechanow to the Narev and formed a bridge-head on the left bank. The Pomorze Army that had successfully reached its fall back defen-sive positions was now threatened from the south by fast moving German forces.

On Wednesday September 6 the XVI and XV Panzer Corps punched through the Prusy Army at Tomaszow and fought their way towards Warsaw. The 22nd Army Corps under von Kleist had reached Tarnow and the Polish defence line had been split open between Czestochowa and Warsaw.

A day later Marshal Rydz-Smigly aban-doned his headquarters in Warsaw and moved eastwards to Brest-Litovsk.

German assessments of Polish options were not to try and hold the Vistula but attempt to hold a line behind the Narev, Vistula and San while concentrating about seven to ten divisions around Lublin.

The OKH, *Oberkommando des Heeres* –

LEFT: Waffen-SS troops in action in a village. One takes aim with a M1912 Mauser Military "Broomhandle" automatic pistol.

Right: German soldiers prepare a message carrying Alsatian dog. Dogs were used in the war to locate casualties, find mines and even by the Russians as living anti-tank mines.

BELOW: Marshal Rydz-Smigly the Polish C-in-C, the first victim of *Blitzkrieg* tactics.

Army High Command – ordered Army Group North under General Fedor von Bock to send the 3rd Army across the Narev on the axis Siedlce-Warsaw while the 4th Army advanced along the Vistula.

Meanwhile Army Group South was ordered to encircle to cut off the Lodz Army to prevent it taking a stand on the Vistula and allow the 14th Army to attack Lublin from the south.

The next three days became a race for the Vistula as Polish forces attempted to keep cohesion under air attacks and the pressure of German armoured columns who succeeded in splitting up the Polish combat groups and cut deep into the Polish defence lines.

By Friday the German forces had penetrated the southwest suburbs of Warsaw and cut off the Pomorze, Poznan, Lodz, Cracow and elements of the Prusy Armies from a withdrawal route. The main elements of the German 10th Army encircled the southern group of the Prusy Army at Radom and reached the Vistula, while the spearheads of the 4th Panzer Division under General Reinhardt were in front of the battered but defiant city of Warsaw.

The fighting had lasted a week and the Poles were hard pressed but were still retaining cohesion as they withdrew.

WEEK TWO

The disintegration and surrender of the scattered or encircled remnants of the Polish Army is proceeding rapidly...Hostilities have resumed outside Warsaw after the Polish truce delegate failed to turn up. The Poles are defending the city without thought for the population of over one million.
OKW Communiqué September 19, 1939

On Saturday September 9, 1939 the OKH ordered the German 8th Army to accelerate its advance towards Warsaw to cut off the Pomorze and Poznan Armies which were withdrawing in contact with the tanks and infantry of the 4th Army.

Meanwhile in the south the Carpathian Army was forced back from its positions on the River Dunajec towards Przemysl.

Initial probes into Warsaw by tanks of the

ABOVE: Germans soldiers nervously scan the ruins of Warsaw for snipers.

RIGHT: House clearing German style, breaking into a building in Warsaw.

4th Panzer Division met with tough resistance in the suburbs and after three hours the Germans withdrew after losing 57 of the 120 tanks they had committed.

On September 10, the 3rd Army and the XVI Panzer Corps had trapped ten Polish divisions around Modlin. The Polish force was made up of elements of the Pomorze Army and the Poznan Army that was almost intact. A desperate battle now opened between the Germans and the Poznan and Pomorze Armies trying to break out of encirclement across the River Bzura where they managed to capture bridgeheads near Lowicz.

The Poznan Army attacked in a south east direction against the advancing German 8th Army. The OKH had lost contact with the two

Polish armies and initially the attack was a shock. In a three day battle at Kutno the Poles virtually destroyed the 30th Infantry Division commanded by Major General von Briesen and forced the Germans back 16km (10 miles) before, supported by air attacks in vicious fighting near Lowicz and Sochaczew, reinforcements from the German 10th Army checked the attack.

BELOW: Flames roar from a building in a Polish village as German soldiers carrying respirators and assault equipment scan the streets.

RIGHT: Shells or bombs have set fire to this house, silhouetting the German troops dashing through the streets to clear the village.

On September 10 the left flank of Army Group North attacked south and south east across the River Narev encircling the bulk of the Polish Narev Operational Group under General Mlot-Fijalkowski at Zambrowo. At the industrial city of Radom on the bend of Vistula fighting had reached a crescendo.

On the same day to the south the 14th Army established bridgeheads across the River San on either side of Przemysl. Meanwhile to the north Guderian's XIX Panzer Corps had carved its way through the Narev Operational Group and annihilated the Polish 18th Infantry at Lomza. When the XIX Panzer Corps reached Brest Litovsk the Polish high command realised that they would be unable to move the front to establish positions behind the River Bug.

Monday September 11 marked the day when the cohesive Polish resistance began to collapse. The XV and XVI Panzer Corps and the 4th Army Corps had encircled the Prusy Army at Radom and its commander General Dab-Biernacki along with 60,000 soldiers was forced to surrender. To the north on the same day the 1st Army Corps severed the Poles eastward communications with Warsaw.

Despite the breakdown of command and control the Poles were far from beaten. On September 11 the Army of Poznan continued its attacks from Bzura towards Strykow, but General Kutrzeba realised that these attacks were making no headway and so shifted his army to the lower Bzura and then thrust eastward to open a path to Warsaw. He believed that this new unexpected axis might catch the enemy around Lodz by surprise.

The 4th Army Corps commanded by

LEFT: A Waffen-SS MG34 crew with their machine gun mounted on a Dreifuss 34 AA tripod take aim at a ground target. Opening the bipod helped to give the weapon a better centre of gravity on this mount.

RIGHT: Polish artillerymen prepare to ride into action with their howitzer. The Polish Army was modernising its weapons and equipment in 1939.

General von Schwedler formed weak bridge-heads across the Vistula at Annapol and Solec on September 14. The ad hoc formation of the Lublin Army was now in no condition to oppose them. The major threat was however to the south where the 14th Army had crossed the River San, reached Lvov and so cut off a withdrawal route to the south east for the Carpathian Army and any other Polish forces that might attempt to escape to Hungary and Romania. When the 22nd Army Corps under General von Kleist reached Hrubieszow they cut off the Cracow Army from the south and also blocked withdrawal routes into the hills around Lublin.

The following day the 14th Army was ordered to advance towards Tarnopol and Stanislawow to block retreat routes to Romania which was still neutral.

The converging German armies had surrounded Warsaw by September 15 and demanded that the city surrender. It refused and was subject to what at the time was seen as a massive air attack.

On Saturday September 16 von Rundstedt started the final encirclement of the Armies of Poznan and Pomorze. The battered divisions of the Army of Poznan managed to fight through to the lower Bzura, but the Army of Pomorze was cut off and trapped in the confluence of the Rivers Vistula and Bzura.

In a letter home a soldier of the *Leibstandarte-Adolf Hitler* later recalled the shock of war.

"Our advance took us across that part of the battlefield which had been held by the so-called Pomorze Army. The whole area was a scene of death and destruction. The bloated bodies of men and animals blackening under the hot sun, smashed carts, burnt out vehicles and those most tragic victims of war, the wounded horses, waiting for the mercy shot. Everywhere there was evidence of a beaten army covering the ground.

"Now I understand what the words of our song mean:

'Man and horse and wagon, the Lord God struck them all down...'"

THE STAB IN THE BACK

"The Soviet Union can no longer remain indifferent to the sufferings of its blood-brothers the Ukrainians and Belorussians who, inhabitants of Polish territory, are being abandoned to their fate and left defenceless. In consideration of this situation the Soviet Government has ordered the Red Army to send its troops across the frontier to take under their protection the lives and welfare of the populations of western Ukraine and western Belorussia."

Vladimir Potemkin,
Soviet Deputy Commissar for Foreign Affairs
03.00 September 17, 1939

The Soviet Union attacked Poland on Sunday September 17 and the Polish government fled across the border into Romania, but was interned following Soviet pressure. The invading Soviet forces consisted of the Belorussian Front (Army Group) under General Kovalev made up of the Vitebsk, Bobruisk, 10th and 11th Armies and to the south the Ukrainian Front under General Timoshenko composed of the Zhitomir, Vinnitsa and 12th Armies. The Pripet Marshes that divided the two Fronts proved no obstacle to their advance.

Committed to their fight to the death in the west the Polish forces were in no condition to offer a coherent resistance though they hung onto the important rail junction of Moledeczno on the line between Minsk and Vilna. In the first day's fighting the Red Air Force reported that it had shot down seven Polish fighters and three bombers and the Army said that its troops "were greeted with cheers by the local White Russian and Ukrainian populations".

The surviving 116 aircraft of the *Lotnictwo Wojskowe* flew into Romania where they were interned.

On that grim Sunday the XIX Panzer Corps

ABOVE: A German NCO swigs from his water bottle in the heat of the autumn sun.

RIGHT: The crew of a Polish Bofors 40mm medium anti-aircraft gun scan the sky. The Poles had limited AA defences.

under Guderian drove along the right bank of the Vistula, seized Wlodawa and formed a bridgehead on the left bank of the Bug. His reconnaissance and advanced forces had reached the Lublin-Kovel railway and so cut off Polish forces on the northern front from retreat behind the Bug.

Meanwhile the 4th Army Corps advancing from the Annapol area on the axis Krasnik – Krasnystaw – Lublin cut the Polish Army of Lublin in half while the 14th Army blocked routes to the south.

The 14th Army was now aligned west along the line Zamosc – Tomaszow – Lubelski. Its centre then pushed towards Lvov encountering violent resistance and was attacked from the rear by elements of the Army of the Carpathians. The Poles had been encircled

ABOVE: Hitler scans the front through artillery observers' periscope binoculars. He would gloat over France less than a year later but as the war swung against the Third Reich his visits to the front became infrequent.

after evacuating Przemysl and were now attempting to push towards Lvov.

The remnants of the Army of Pomorze finally surrendered between September 18 – 19 inside the Bzura pocket. The remains of the Army of Poznan fought their way through to Warsaw. By now the capital had a garrison of 180,000. However few were adequately armed.

Units of von Reichenau's 10th Army and List's 14th Army surrounded the 60,000 strong Army of Lublin on Wednesday

September 20 and its commander General Pyskor was forced to surrender.

On September 21 Soviet troops reached Lvov. The garrison under General Langner put up a tough resistance for ten days before being obliged to surrender. Soviet forces finally halted on the north south line of the Rivers San and Bug. When Soviet forces linked up with the German 4th Army at Brest-Litovsk on September 18 the German News Bureau reported smugly "On Monday, German and Soviet troop detachments rendezvoused at Brest-Litovsk: the officers exchanged greetings".

Hitler entered Danzig in triumph and made a seemingly conciliatory speech directed at Britain and France on September 19.

Heavy air raids were directed against Warsaw on Sunday September 24 to prepare the way for the ground forces of von Küchler's 3rd Army and von Reichenau's 10th Army who were to attack the following day.

Surviving Polish forces began to fight their way towards Romania and Hungary, coun-tries that at the time were still neutral and eventually some 120,000 managed to escape to serve with the Allies.

Warsaw capitulated on September 27, and on the same day Hitler summoned his generals to a conference in Berlin and told them that he planned to invade France and demanded to know how long it would take for them to prepare for the attack.

Ten Polish divisions trapped near Modlin north of Warsaw were finally forced to

ABOVE: A young Polish soldier takes aim through the fork of a tree. He carries the pack, blanket and shovel that make up full marching order, a burden for men going into action.

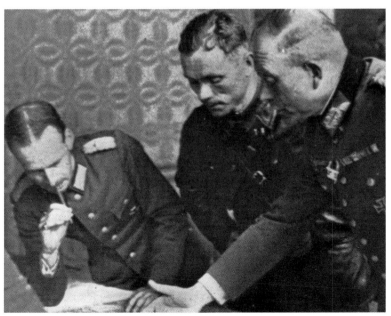

LEFT: General Guderian discusses boundaries with a Soviet tank officer following the link up between German and Russian forces in eastern Poland.

surrender on September 28. By now German and Soviet troops had reached the demarcation line that split Poland in two. A day later von Ribbentrop and Molotov met in Moscow to modify the non-aggression pact between the two countries. It was agreed that the Soviet Union would be given a free hand in Lithuania and would retain Belorussia and Ukrainian Poland. In exchange Germany was given the whole of ethnic Poland.

In Paris on September 30 General Wladyslaw Sikorski formed a government in exile. He later formed an army from Polish expatriates and soldiers who had escaped. It was initially under French command and later the surviving 20,000 men served with distinction with the British Army. They would fight heroically in North Africa and Europe.

ABOVE: The victory parade in Warsaw. The perfect drill by men who had been in action only days earlier is almost a visual metaphor for German military efficiency.

When the fighting ended on the coast three Polish destroyers and two submarines slipped past the *Kriegsmarine* blockade on October 1 and eventually escaped to Great Britain. The 4,000 men of the Polish Navy on the tiny Hel peninsula commanded by Rear-Admiral Unrug surrendered that day.

The last vestige of resistance in Poland ended by October 5. Among the units that kept up the fight to the last was a mixed squadron of unarmed RWD Model 8 and PWS 26 training/liaison aircraft. The pilots were still attacking German ground troops with

Above: The Führer greets his victors. There would be more triumphs in the next three years feeding an illusion of invincibility that would perish in the snows of Russia.

hand grenades they threw from their cockpits in a final gesture of defiance.

On Friday October 6 Hitler visited the men of the 8th Army outside Warsaw and ordered a parade of the men who had taken part in the fighting in the Polish capital. The OKW reported that morning that the last remnants of the Polish army, approximately 8,000 men under General Kleeberg, surrendered at Kock east of Deblin.

The campaign had cost the Germans 8,082 killed, 27,278 wounded and 5,029 missing. Compared to the grim butcher's bill of World War I these losses seemed minute. The Soviet Union lost 737 dead and 1,859 wounded.

The Poles lost 70,000 killed and 130,000 wounded while the survivors marched into grim captivity. They had been unable to mobilise their full strength from September 1 and so had only 540,000 men and 160 tanks in the field. Crucially they had been let down by Anglo French forces in the West.

At the close of the campaign in Poland Guderian derived considerable satisfaction from the report that at one time only 25 per cent of German vehicles were out of action through mechanical problems. The *Panzerwaffe* had come a long way from the unreliable vehicles that had crawled into Austria only eighteen months before.

After action analysis established that the

ABOVE: Under international supervision the bodies of Polish officers shot by the Russians at Katyn in 1939 are disinterred for identification in April 1943. The crime, not-untypical of the Soviet Union under Stalin, would test the cohesion of the Allies.

performance of the Light Divisions had been disappointing, they had neither the clout of an armoured division, nor the numbers of an infantry division or motorised rifle division.

After Poland Panzer divisions were each assigned a *Luftwaffe* liaison unit with its own signals vehicles to maintain contact with supporting bombers and fighters.

Following the defeat of Poland both Germany and the USSR made considerable efforts to exterminate the Polish political, military and intellectual leadership. In the woods in the Ukraine at Katyn close to Smolensk the Soviet secret police killed 4,500 Polish officers they had captured. In April 1943 the Germans found the mass graves in the woods. The prisoners' hands had been bound and they had been shot in the back of the head at close range. A neutral commission examined the site and agreed with the Germans that these were the bodies of men captured in 1939 by the Red Army when it invaded eastern Poland. In addition to these murders the Soviet Union deported almost 1,700,000 Poles to Siberia.

In western Poland as the invasion was still underway the Germans instituted the *Ausserordentliche Befriedungsaktion* – the Extraordinary Pacification Action or AD Aktion – on the orders of the Governor-General of Poland Hans Frank and his deputy

OBERKOMMANDO DES HEERES (OKH) ORDER OF NOVEMBER 13, 1939

Re: Informing family members of casualties:
We have cause to point out that the process of informing people of casualties to their families (deaths, missing-in-action, severe wounds) must be carried out in a fitting manner. A few personal words and an acknowledgement of the achievements of the deceased, missing or wounded person are particularly comforting.

Artur Seyss-Inquart. Under their direction between September 1939 and June 1940, 2,000 Polish men and women were apprehended and executed. The first execution of 107 men took place in Wawer, a town near Warsaw, on December 27, 1939.

They were the first of about three million who would die. During the war Poland lost 45 per cent of her doctors, 57 per cent of her lawyers, 40 per cent of her academics, 30 per cent of her engineers, 185 of her clergy and most of her journalists. The Germans deported approximately 2,000,000 Polish men and women for forced labour in the Reich and Occupied France working in factories, farms or on defences.

On Sunday October 1, 1939 the British Prime Minister Winston Churchill broadcasting to the world summed up the feelings of the West. "Poland has again been overrun by two of the great Powers which held her in bondage for 150 years, but were unable to quench the spirit of the Polish nation. The heroic defence of Warsaw shows that the soul of Poland is indestructible, and that she will rise again like a rock which may for a spell be submerged by a tidal wave, but which remains a rock."

sIG 33

The sIG 33 was a SP howitzer that equipped German infantry battalions. It combined the 15cm Infantry Gun with a PzKpfw I chassis. Though it was a rather clumsy, top heavy and underpowered design it was a very effective vehicle in 1939-40. In 1942 the gun was mounted on a PzKpfw II chassis and finally on a PzKpfw III.

SPECIFICATIONS

Armament:	One 15cm sIG 33 howitzer
Armour:	6-13mm (0.23-0.51in)
Crew:	4
Weight:	11,505kg (11.32tons)
Hull length:	4.85m (15ft 10in)
Width:	2.15m (7ft 0.6in)
Height:	2.40m (7ft 10.5in)
Engine:	Praga 6-cylinder, petrol, 150bhp.
Road speed:	35km/h (21.75mph)
Range:	185km (115miles

FALL WESERÜBUNG

The basic aim is to lend the operation the character of a peaceful occupation, designed to protect by force of arms the neutrality of the Northern countries...Any resistance which is nevertheless offered will be broken by all means available.

Führer Directive 10a March 1, 1940

On Wednesday November 29, 1939 the USSR attacked Finland. The Soviet leader Joseph Stalin had already established with the Nazi foreign minister Joachim von Ribbentrop that the Baltic States of Latvia, Lithuania and Estonia were in the Soviet sphere of influence. In October 1939 a "mutual assistance pact" was agreed between the USSR and Latvia. In June 1940, while the world watched the German invasion of the West, the USSR effortlessly gathered up the three tiny states.

Finland however was a different customer. Stalin saw the close proximity of the Finnish

ABOVE: Curiosity draws Danish women and children to German vehicles following the invasion.

border to Leningrad, the second city of the USSR, as a threat. He offered a mutual assistance treaty and demanded that Finland cede areas of the Karelian Isthmus close to Leningrad. Finland refused on both counts and without warning the USSR attacked.

Finland had a peacetime army of barely 30,000 men grouped in nine divisions composed of three infantry regiments. Finland had 60 largely obsolete tanks, 150 aircraft and 22 anti-aircraft guns.

In the bitter winter of 1939 – 40, reserves were mobilised and 15 Finnish divisions went into action inflicting heavy defeats on 45 Soviet divisions. At Suomussalmi in Karelia on January 5, 1940 outnumbered Finnish ski troops of the 9th Division under Colonel Siilasvuo counter-attacked the Soviet 163rd and 44th Divisions and destroyed them. The Soviet forces lost 27,500 men killed or frozen

to death, 50 tanks as well as artillery and vehicles. The Finnish casualties were 900 dead and 1,770 wounded.

In Germany officers in the OKW noted the incompetent performance of the Soviet divisions and their poor equipment.

The Soviet 10th and 20th Heavy Tank Brigades equipped with multi-turreted T-28 also suffered heavy losses from the small number of Finnish anti-tank gun crews on the Mannerheim Line. They nicknamed the clumsy vehicles "The Mail Train".

In February 1940 the Allied War Council decided to send a 50,000 strong expeditionary force to support Finland. As it was being assembled the Soviet Union committed more **forces to the attack.**

BA-10

Built on the reinforced chassis of the GAZ-AAA commercial truck the BA-10 first appeared in 1932. It was used in the invasion of Poland by the USSR in 1939 and in 1941 large numbers were captured by the Germans. They used them for anti-partisan operations. Surviving vehicles were stripped down by Soviet engineers and used as armoured- personnel carriers.

SPECIFICATIONS

Armament:	1 x 37mm (1.45in) /45mm (1.77in); 1 x 7.92mm (0.31in) MG
Armour:	25mm (0.98in)
Crew:	4
Weight:	7,500kg (8.267tons)
Hull length:	4.70m (15ft 5in)
Width:	2.09m (6ft 10in)
Height:	2.42m (7ft 11in)
Engine:	GAZ-M 14 cylinder water-cooled petrol developing 85hp
Road speed:	87km/h (54mph)
Range:	320km (199miles)

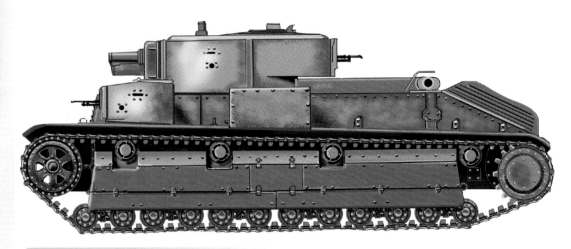

T-28

Though a medium tank, with its three turrets the T-28 developed in 1932 looked to observers in Moscow on the May Day parade superficially like a heavy tank.

It went through four modifications during its production run from 1933 to 1940.

By the time of the Winter War against Finland there were two T-28 Brigades, the 10th and 20th Heavy Tank Brigades. In an attempt to improve the level of defence the frontal armour on the hull and turret was increased from 50mm (1.96in) to 80mm (3.14in) and the rear and sides to 40mm (1.57in) by adding additional "screened armour". The weight increased to 32,510kg (32tons)

SPECIFICATIONS

Armament:	1 x 76.2mm (3in) (70 rounds); 5 x DT machine-guns (7,938 rounds)
Armour:	80mm (3.14in)
Crew:	6
Weight:	28,510kg (27.6tons)
Hull length:	7.44m (24ft 5in)
Width:	2.81m (9ft 2in)
Height:	2.82m (9ft 3in)
Engine:	M-17L V-12 500bhp petrol engine developing 1,400rpm.
Road speed:	37km/h (22mph)
Range:	220km (135miles).

Despite heavy losses between February 1 and 13 the massively reinforced Northwest Front under General Semyon Timoshenko composed of the 7th Army under General Merestokov and 13th Army under General Grendal punched through the defences of the Mannerheim Line that covered the Karelian Isthmus north of Leningrad. Finland was crushed by sheer weight of numbers. The Soviet Union eventually forced her to capitulate on March 12, 1940. The Winter War had cost the Russians 200,000 men, nearly 700

aircraft and 1,600 tanks. The Finns lost 25,000 men and were forced to sign a treaty on March 15, 1940 in which they ceded the city of Viborg, the Karelian Isthmus and other territory.

On February 16, 1940 a boarding party from the destroyer HMS *Cossack* had released 299 British merchant sailors held prisoner aboard the German supply ship KMS *Altmark* sheltering in Jössing Fjord in Norway.

In 1940 Norway was neutral and German

ABOVE: The slim fuselage of the Dornier Do17, the fast medium bomber and reconnaissance aircraft nicknamed the "Flying Pencil".

BELOW: An E Boat on patrol. Ideal for operations in the Baltic these fast torpedo boats would later extend their operations to the Channel.

cargo ships used her ice free port of Narvik to collect high-grade Swedish iron ore for the war industries of the Ruhr. The British considered mining the coastal waters to disrupt this traffic and even making a landing at Narvik. With two *Führer* Directives on February 26 and March 1 Hitler forestalled these moves with Fall N, Case N for North. The invasion plans were given the code name Operation *Weserübung* – Weser Exercise, a name that sounded like a simple river crossing exercise.

Weserübung originally scheduled for March 20 was quite simply the invasion of Denmark and Norway.

The Danes had a tiny Army of 14,000 men.

ABOVE: The smashed hull of the Tribal Class destroyer HMS *Eskimo* hit by bombs off Norway. She limped back to Britain, was rebuilt and survived the war to be scrapped at Troon in Scotland in 1949.

The Royal Danish Navy of 3,000 had submarines, torpedo boats and two elderly coastal defence vessels the *Niels, Juel* and *Peder Skram*. They also manned the forts and coastal defences. The Royal Danish Air Force had 50 mostly obsolete aircraft.

At 04.15 on April 9, 1940 two German motorised brigade groups from the XXXI Corps commanded by General Kaupisch crossed the north German border with

ABOVE: Smoke rises above Oslo airport as Ju52 transport aircraft shuttle in German troops in the near bloodless take over of the Norwegian capital.

RIGHT: German mountain troops with an MG34 on an AA mount aboard a small vessel making its way up the Norwegian coast.

Denmark. Assisted by parachute and air landing attacks on the airfields and the key bridges between the islands they quickly overwhelmed the country. The airborne attack at 05.00, history's first parachute attack, secured the unarmed fortress of Madnesø and soon afterwards the important airport of Aalborg in northern Jutland. Captain Gericke commanding 4th Company 1 *Fallschirmjäger* Regiment captured the 3–kilometre (2.175 mile) long bridge linking the Danish islands of Falster and Fünen. By 06.00 Copenhagen was in German hands. The Danish forces had only been able to offer token resistance and suffered 13 killed and 24 wounded. The Danes were obliged to accept the presence of the invaders, however the government remained in place with the courts and police under its control. King

RIGHT: As German forces landed in Norway Norwegian, French and British forces attempted to block their advance. Halted at Lillehammer the Allies were forced back and landings at Namsos were also counter attacked.

GLOSTER GLADIATOR MK 1

The Gloster Gladiator entered service in 1937 and was the last biplane fighter with the RAF and Fleet Air Arm (FAA). Two squadrons, No 263 and No 804 Squadron FAA, flying Gladiators took part in the Norwegian campaign. Some aircraft operated off frozen lake Lesjaskog when airfields were not available or had been bombed. The Sea Gladiator had a catapult point, arrester hook and stowage for a dinghy. When it had been withdrawn from front line service it was used for liaison and meteorological work until 1944.

SPECIFICATIONS
Type:	Single engined fighter
Crew:	1
Power Plant:	One 840hp Bristol Mercury
Performance:	Maximum speed at 4,420m (14,500ft) 407km/h (235mph)
Range:	689km (428miles)
Weights:	Maximum 2,083kg (4,592lb)
Dimensions:	Wing span 9.83m (32ft 3in)
Length:	8.36m (27ft 5in)
Height:	3.63mm (11ft 9in)
Armament:	Two fixed forward firing .303in Browning MGs in fuselage and two Browning or Lewis MGs under lower wings.

LEFT: *Gebirgsjäger* in the snow. German mountain troops trained in Bavaria and Austria and were experts in winter warfare operations and climbing. By 1945 they would have served in Norway, Crete and Russia, in 1942 climbing Mt Elbrus, the highest mountain in Europe.

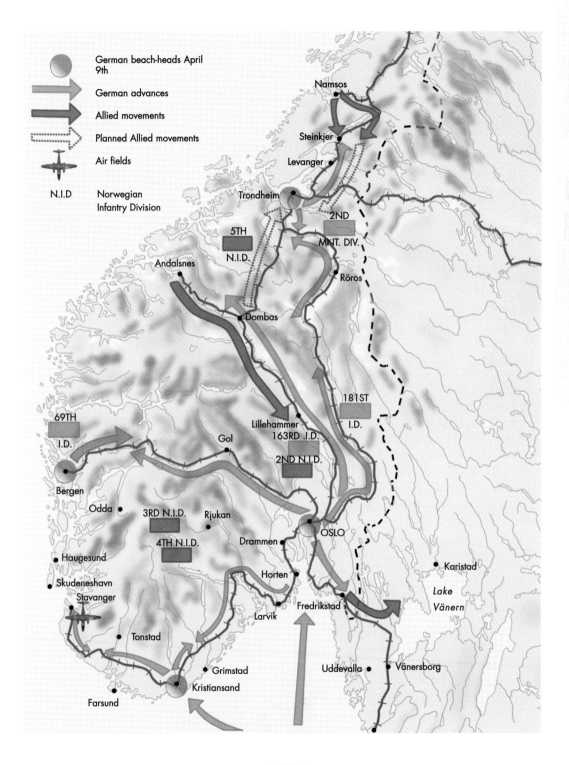

German beach-heads April 9th

German advances

Allied movements

Planned Allied movements

Air fields

N.I.D   Norwegian Infantry Division

Namsos

Steinkjer

Levanger

Trondheim

2ND

5TH
N.I.D.

MNT. DIV.

Andalsnes

Röros

Dombas

181ST
I.D.

69TH
I.D.

Lillehammer
163RD .I.D.

Gol

Bergen

2ND N.I.D.

Odda

3RD N.I.D.

Rjukan

4TH N.I.D.

OSLO

Drammen

Haugesund

Karistad

Skudeneshavn

Horten

Stavanger

Fredrikstad

*Lake
Vänern*

Larvik

Tonstad

Grimstad

Uddevalla

Vänersborg

Kristiansand

Farsund

Frederik IX who remained in the country provided a focus for loyalty and until August 1943 the government retained some degree of independence.

Denmark was effectively a stepping stone for the Germans for the invasion of Norway. The German forces intended for this operation, commanded by Colonel General Niklaus von Falkenhorst, were divided into five groups.

Group I with ten destroyers carrying the 139th *Gebirgsjäger* Regiment were to land at Narvik in the north. Group II with the heavy cruiser KMS *Hipper* and four destroyers delivered the 138th *Gebirgsjäger* Regiment to Trondheim. Group III composed of two battalions of the 69th Division would land at

ABOVE: A 2cm Flak 30 AA gun with range finder covers German shipping in a Norwegian fjord. The gun had a maximum vertical range of 2,000 metres and could be depressed for use against ground targets.

RIGHT: Endless columns of German troops march into Oslo watched by small crowds.

Bergen from the light cruisers KMS *Köln* and KMS *Königsberg*, the Gunnery Training ship KMS *Bremse* and the depot ship KMS *Karl Peters*. Group IV at Kristians and Arendal composed of one battalion of the 310th Regiment was to land from the light cruiser KMS *Karlsruhe* and the depot ship KMS *Tsingtau*. Group V made up of two battalions

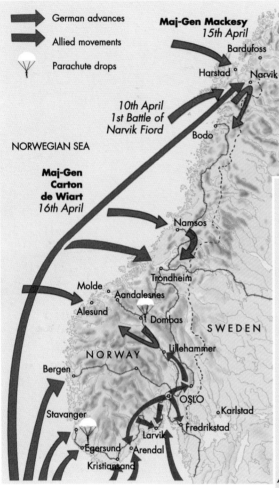

German advances

Allied movements

Parachute drops

Maj-Gen Mackesy
15th April

Bardufoss

Harstad   Narvik

10th April
1st Battle of
Narvik Fiord

Bodo

NORWEGIAN SEA

Maj-Gen
Carton
de Wiart
16th April

Namsos

Trondheim

Molde   Aandalesnes

Alesund   Dombas

SWEDEN

Lillehammer

NORWAY

Bergen

OSLO

Stavanger   Karlstad

Larvik   Fredrikstad

Egersund   Arendal

Kristiansand

LEFT: German airborne and naval forces effectively secured southern Norway in a series of landings. Though the Royal Navy was a far more powerful force than the Kriegsmarine the Germans had the advantage of superior air power which they used very effectively to move troops and attack enemy concentrations.

German advances

Allied retreats

Bardufoss

Harstad   Narvik

NORWEGIAN SEA

June 3–8   Bodo

May 4–18

May 2–10

May 2   Namsos

Trondheim

April 30th   Molde

Aandalesnes   Roros

Alesund

Dombas   SWEDEN

NORWAY

Lillehammer

Bergen

Odda   Rjukan

Haugesund   Drammen   OSLO

Horten   Karlstad

Stavanger

Tonstad   Larvik

Grimstad

Egersund   Kristiansand

RIGHT: Under pressure on the ground and in the air the Allies were forced to withdraw, though the Norwegian King and the country's gold reserves were safely evacuated to Britain from Andalsnes aboard the cruiser HMS *Devonshire*. Only in the north at Narvik were the Germans suffering losses on land and particularly at sea.

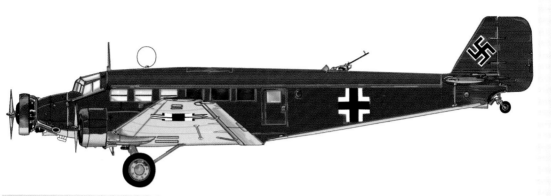

JUNKERS JU52/3M G7E

The rugged "Tante Ju" – Auntie Junkers – with its distinctive corrugated fuselage was the transport workhorse for the *Luftwaffe* throughout the war. A total of 4,850 were built and ironically the largest operator of the type after the Germans was the USSR that had over 80 captured or repaired aircraft. The USAAF had one Ju52 that they gave the designation C-79 and the RAF had two. It was aboard Ju52s that German paratroops were carried to Crete in the assault in 1941.

SPECIFICATIONS
Type:	Three engined medium transport
Crew:	3/18 troops/12 stretchers
Power Plant:	One Three 830hp BMW 132T-2
Performance:	Maximum speed at 1,400 m (4,590ft)
	286 km/h (178mph)
Normal range:	1,500km (930miles)
Weights:	Empty 6,560kg (14,462lb)
	Loaded 11,030kg (24,320lb)
Dimensions:	Wing span 29.24m (95ft 11in)
Length:	18.9m (62ft)
Armament:	One 7.92mm (0.31in) MG 15 in
	open aft dorsal position lower wings.

of the 163rd Division would land at Oslo, the Norwegian capital, where they would be assisted by airborne forces. The Oslo Group would be supported by the pocket battleship KMS *Lützow* (formerly the *Deutschland*), the heavy cruiser KMS *Blücher* and light cruiser KMS *Emden*.

They would be backed by the X *Fliegerkorps* commanded by Lt General Hans Geissler with 290 bombers, 40 Stukas, 100 fighters and 70 floatplanes. In addition the Luftwaffe corps had 500 Ju52 transports that allowed troops and equipment to be moved across mountain ridges or deep fjords.

Norway, like Finland, was not a nation prepared to accept invasion and though her

forces were not fully mobilised they put up a tough and very creditable resistance. The peacetime strength of the Norwegian Army was six divisions that would on mobilisation be expanded to a force of 56,000. The bulk of the divisions were concentrated in the south, the 1st, 2nd, 3rd and 4th close to the capital Oslo, while the 5th was based near Trondheim and the 6th at Narvik.

The Navy that had been partially mobilised in 1939 had four new escort destroyers, a new minelayer, two large but outmoded coastal defence vessels, three small pre-1918 destroyers and about 40 smaller vessels. The coastal forts partially manned and the naval air force brought the total mobilised

manpower of the navy to 5,000.

The Air Force had 40 aircraft, only 16 of which were modern and the navy had six modern and about 20 older types.

One of the first and most dramatic acts of resistance was by the coastal defence batteries at Oscarborg and in the Dröbak Narrows who acting on their own initiative opened fire on the German warships under command of Rear Admiral Oskar Kummetz and then launched a pattern of torpedoes. Two hit and sank the modern 13,000 ton heavy cruiser KMS *Blücher* in Dröbak fjord. The pocket battleship KMS *Lützow* was also damaged and forced to turn back. The ships had come into range as they carried troops and equipment to land at Oslo. The illustrated multilingual Nazi propaganda magazine *Signal* would later feature the operation in

ABOVE AND RIGHT: German infantry from Group V ride in freight trucks as a train carries them deeper into Norway. Ships, aircraft and trains were used by the invaders to cross the rugged terrain.

dramatic three-dimensional maps that even showed the loss of *Blücher*. Germany was after all at war and losses are inevitable – an acceptable price for final victory. Germany was now conquering whole countries for the sort of losses that would have been incurred in a fruitless offensive on the Western Front in World War I.

The men of Group V led by Major General Erwin Engelbrecht managed to land at Oslo, seized half of the city and crucially Fornebu airfield. Early on the afternoon of April 9 Ju52 transports began to fly in reinforcements.

RIGHT: Following the destruction of their shipping in two attacks by the Royal Navy the German forces at Narvik were forced back against the Swedish border and were close to defeat in the spring of 1940.

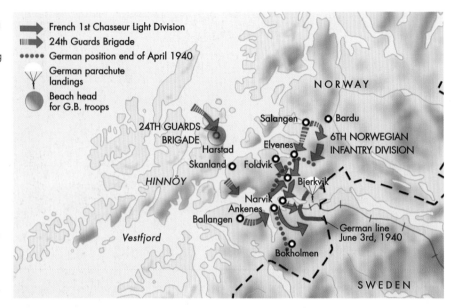

French 1st Chasseur Light Division
24th Guards Brigade
German position end of April 1940
German parachute landings
Beach head for G.B. troops

NORWAY

24TH GUARDS BRIGADE
Harstad
Skanland
Foldvik
HINNÖY
Bjerkvik
Narvik
Ankenes
Ballangen
Vestfjord
Bokholmen

Salangen
Elvenes
Bardu
6TH NORWEGIAN INFANTRY DIVISION

German line June 3rd, 1940

SWEDEN

LEFT: A Ju52 circles above *Fallschirmjäger* on the Narvik drop zone as reinforcements are parachuted in.

ABOVE: German gunners man a captured Norwegian coastal defence gun covering the approaches to Oslo.

LEFT: A *Gebirgsjäger* with a Solothurn MG30 light machine gun. A special trigger allowed single shots or bursts to be fired.

At Bergen the light cruiser KMS *Königsberg* was crippled by two 210mm shells fired by a coastal battery. Unable to put to sea she was sunk by aircraft of the Fleet Air Arm on April 11. Earlier naval actions offshore should have given the Norwegian government warning that the country was about to be attacked. On the morning of April 8 the Polish submarine *Orzel* had sunk the German transport *Rio de Janeiro* off Kristiansand and the survivors had told the Norwegians that they were the first wave of troops that the *Führer* was sending to the aid of Norway.

The delays imposed by the defences on the German task force at Oslo gave King Haakon VII and the Norwegian Royal family enough time to escape. Eventually they went via Andalsnes to Great Britain taking with them the Norwegian gold reserves aboard the cruiser HMS *Devonshire*. A Norwegian Government in exile headed by the King was established in London on May 5.

Earlier King Haakon had refused to accept a government headed by the Norwegian Nazi Vidkun Quisling stating that he would rather abdicate than endorse the Norwegian traitor.

On April 8 the men of the 13,900 ton heavy cruiser KMS *Admiral Hipper* encountered the 1,345 ton destroyer HMS *Glowworm* commanded by Lieutenant Commander

FALL WESERÜBUNG

VIDKUN QUISLING

The man whose name would become a by-word for treachery was born in Fyresdal, Telemarken on July 18, 1887. Lauritz Vidkun Abraham Quisling, the future leader of the Norwegian Fascist National Union Party, graduated from the Norwegian Military Academy as a junior officer in 1911. Between 1922 and 1926 he worked with Fridtjof Nansen, the scientist and Polar explorer. Entering politics he became Foreign Minister in 1931. Two years later he established the Fascist *Nasjonal Samling* party, at this time Fascism enjoyed a considerable following in Europe since it was seen as a force to combat Communism and sustain national and religious values in the face of an international and atheistic philosophy. However the liberal tradition in Norway produced only 10,000 party members. Following the German invasion in 1940 Quisling declared himself Prime Minister and on February 1, 1942 he was made Minister President by the Reich Commissioner for Norway, Josef Terboven. He quarrelled with Terboven, took sharp measures against his opponents and collaborated in the round up of Jews.

After the war he surrendered to the newly restored Norwegian government, was arrested, tried, found guilty of treason and shot in Oslo on October 24, 1945. His conduct during the war did much to distract the Norwegian public from addressing the responsibility of the President Nygaardsvold, Foreign Minister Dr Halvdan Koht and Defence Minister Ljunborg for the country's lack of preparedness in 1940.

Gerard Roope. The destroyer had become detached from escorting the battle cruiser HMS *Renown* off Norway during a search for a man lost overboard. In a short but heroic action the German sailors watched as under heavy fire the destroyer closed the range with the cruiser and rammed her before finally sinking. The damaged warship was forced to return to Germany, but only one officer and 30 crew members of *Glowworm* survived. Roope was awarded a posthumous Victoria Cross. Dramatic photographs taken from aboard the Admiral Hipper appeared in *Signal*, an indisputable record of heroism of the captain and crew of the destroyer.

The German forces who had landed at Oslo pushed inland and linked up with Group II

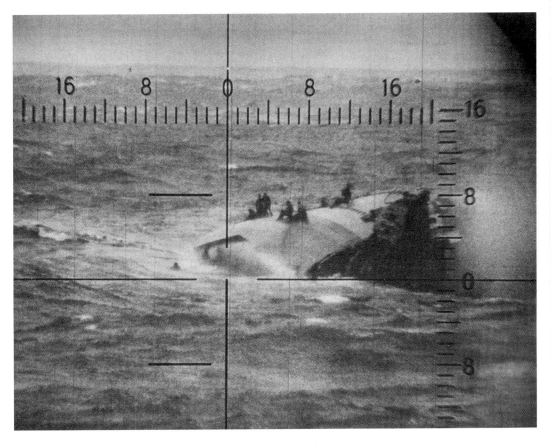

LEFT: A German diagram shows how KMS *Admiral Hipper* manoeuvred to avoid the torpedoes fired by the destroyer HMS *Glowworm*. The ship then went on to ram the cruiser.

ABOVE: Following the attack on April 18 some of the 30 survivors, seen through a gun sight on *Hipper*, cling to the sinking remains of HMS *Glowworm*.

and III. Southern Norway passed under German control by April 16. However in the north the French, Polish and British forces that had originally been intended for Finland were landed near Narvik on April 15, a day later at Namsos and on April 18 at Andalsnes. Allied operational responsibility for Norway was split between Lt General Massy commanding Allied Forces Central Norway and North Norway under Admiral Lord Cork and Orrery.

At Andalsnes the British 148th Brigade commanded by Brigadier Morgan pushed inland along the line of the railway to Oslo and at Lillehammer encountered the German 163rd Infantry Division and was forced back. The Allies evacuated the port on April 30.

The Anglo French 146th Brigade that landed at Namsos was commanded by the dashing Major General Carton de Wiart VC. Wounded in World War I he now sported a piratical black eye patch. It was persuaded by the Norwegian commander General Ruge to move south to assist Norwegian troops

RENAULT R-35

Developed in the mid-1930s to replace the World War I vintage Renault FT 17. By 1940 1,600 had been built. The tank was slow and underpowered and the dumpy 37mm Modèle 1916 gun was not powerful enough to penetrate the armour of most German tanks. The French took R-35s to Narvik where some were abandoned after the fighting. Tanks captured in France were used by the Germans as ammunition carriers, artillery tractors or for SP guns. The turrets were removed and incorporated into bunkers in the Atlantic Wall.

Armament:	1 x 37mm (1.45in);
	1 x 7.5mm (0.29in) MG
Armour:	40mm (1.57in)
Crew:	2
Weight:	10,000kg (9.84tons)
Hull length:	4.20m (13ft 9in)
Width:	1.85m (6ft)
Height:	2.37m (7ft 9in)
Engine:	Renault 4-cylinder petrol
	developing 82hp
Road speed:	20km/h (12.4mph)
Range:	140km (87miles)

RIGHT: *Fallschirmjäger* of the 1st Bn 1st Parachute Rgt (FJR 1) gather at the Bjornfjell ski resort above Narvik.

holding Lillehammer but was forced back. French 5th *Demi-Brigade Chasseurs Alpins* arrived on April 24 but were unable to halt the withdrawal and the port was evacuated on May 2.

At Narvik the German forces surprised the elderly coastal defence ships *Eidsvold* and *Norge* and landed, obtaining the surrender of

Colonel Konrad Sundlo, a Quisling. However in two naval actions on April 9 and April 13, 1940 the Royal Navy had attacked destroyers and cargo ships. The British accounted for nine destroyers and seven transports including the German ammunition ship KMS *Rauenfels* that blew up. In the first attack the Royal Navy had suffered losses including the

ABOVE: Ju52s fly in formation from a base in Germany. The tough versatile aircraft would serve throughout the war in parachute assault and evacuation and resupply operations.

BELOW: A Luftwaffe ground controller waves a Swastika flag to delineate the drop zone for an incoming transport aircraft at Narvik. Flags were used signal to bombers and transport aircraft and mark the limit of an advance.

RIGHT: Immaculate in his blue grey *Luftwaffe* service dress a *Fallschirmjäger* officer with FJR 1 addresses his men following their landing.

destroyer HMS *Hardy* and the death of its Captain and the commander of the 2nd Destroyer Flotilla, Captain B. A .W. Warburton-Lee, who was awarded a posthumous VC.

In the second attack the Royal Navy came back in force with the battleship HMS *Warspite* as well as destroyers and sank the remaining German ships commanded by Commodore Paul Bonte. There was jubilation in Paris and London as the Germans under *Generaloberst* Eduard Dietl were now trapped in Narvik.

The German soldiers and sailors were reinforced by parachute troops including men of the 137th *Gebirgsjäger* Regiment who had received a crash parachute course. The 2,600 sailors now trapped ashore were equipped with 8,000 rifles and 325 machine guns taken from the Norwegian Army 6th Division depot at *Elvegardsmoen* and became "Mountain Marines".

A joint French and Polish force commanded by Lt General Claude Auchinleck, who would later serve with distinction in North Africa, landed in the Narvik area between April 28 and May 7. French and Polish troops under General Marie Emile Béthouart grouped as the *1er*

Chasseur Light Division included the 27th *Chasseur Demi-Brigade*, the 13th Foreign Legion *Demi-Brigade* and the 1st Carpathian *Chasseur Demi-Brigade* composed of Polish mountain troops who had escaped in 1939.

The British 24th Guards Brigade under Major General P. J. Mackesy had in fact been in place at Harstad on the offshore island of Hinnöy since April 15, however Mackesy was reluctant to commit it against the German forces. For his lack of initiative he was sacked by Admiral Lord Cork and Orrery.

LEFT: General Eduard Dietl, the victor at Narvik, who was nearly defeated but was saved by events in France in June 1940.

General Béthouart however proved a vigorous commander and while Auchinleck used the 24th Brigade to block the advance by the 2nd *Gebirgsjäger* Division that was attempting to relieve the force at Narvik the French and Poles went into attack. Béthouart pushed the 27th *Demi-Brigade* forward from Elvenes at the end of Gratangerfjord to link up with the Legion forces who had landed at Bjerkvik.

The *Legionnaires* had made an assault landing from landing craft with supporting fire from the battleship HMS *Resolution*, the cruisers HMS *Effingham* and *Vindictive* and five destroyers. It was the first amphibious assault of World War II.

A few days later the Polish forces under General Bohusz-Szyszko relieved the French troops holding the Ankenes ridge that dominated Beisfjord and Narvik. The road to Narvik was open and now, as General Béthouart was making his plans for the final

ABOVE LEFT: A German platoon hunches behind a PzKpfw I as it grinds forward towards a Norwegian town.

ABOVE: The tank accelerates and soldiers run to keep pace. They have blankets strapped to the mess tins on their leather load carrying equipment.

LEFT: Smoke rises from a burning farmhouse as German soldiers move down a snow covered track in Norway.

assault, developments in France and the Low Countries began to force the pace. Auchinleck gave orders that the force should evacuate Narvik but the French general pointed out that this operation would be easier if they defeated the Germans in Narvik.

On May 28 the 13th *Demi-Brigade* of the Foreign Legion with the Norwegian 6th

Division finally captured Narvik – it was the first Allied victory of World War II. The Germans lost ten guns and 150 machine guns and were pushed back into a pocket trapped by the 1st Chasseur Division.

On June 7 the Germans discovered that the Allies had withdrawn as events in France were now making Narvik a side show.

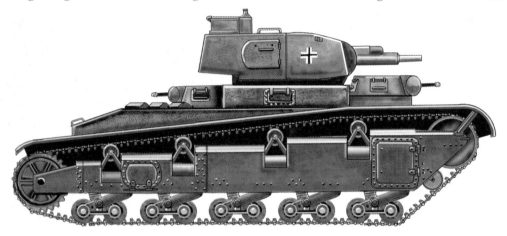

PzKpfw V (Neubaufahrzeug)

This tank designated Panzer V developed from the *Grosstraktor* entered service in 1935. It reflected the idea that an "independent" tank with several gun and machine gun turrets could operate like a land-based warship as part of a break-through force. The British pioneered the concept and it was copied by France, Germany (in secret) and the USSR. The only independent tanks to see action were Soviet medium and heavy designs in 1941. Only three PzKpfw V were built and these were sent to Norway and photographed in Oslo – causing Allied intelligence officers considerable concern. One tank was destroyed in Norway and the survivors became ornaments at the German Panzer School.

Armament:	1 x 7.5cm L/24 (2.95in) (80 rounds), 1 x 3.7cm (1.45in) (50 rounds) and 3 x 7.92mm (0.31in) MG (6,000 rounds)
Armour:	20mm (0.78in)
Crew:	6
Weight:	23,410kg (23.04 tons)
Hull length:	6.60m (21ft 8in)
Width:	2.19m (7ft 2in)
Height:	2.98m (9ft 9in)
Engine:	BMW, 6-cylinder, petrol 250bhp
Road speed:	30km/h (18mph)
Range:	120km (75miles)

RIGHT: A German "Marine", a sailor from a sunken destroyer with Norwegian leather equipment and tunic. These men fought at Narvik and would later qualify for the Narvik Shield.

ABOVE: A wartime map from the magazine *Signal* shows how ships and aircraft were used to move troops to Norway in *Fall Weserübung*. The invasion was described as a pre-emptive move to prevent British forces taking over Norway.

However before they departed they demolished the town's port installations and ore handling facilities.

In Berlin the OKW had considered ordering their force to cross in Sweden to accept internment in this neutral neighbour rather than face surrender. Hitler ordered that they should hold on. His "stand and fight" order saved the day and would become his panacea for grave tactical situations later in the war where withdrawal or manoeuvre was the correct and humane course.

Resistance in Norway ended on June 9, 1940 with an armistice signed by Major-General Otto Ruge for the Norwegian Army. Norwegian soldiers were allowed to go home, as were Norwegian professional officers who undertook not to take up arms against the Third Reich. Ruge refused to make this undertaking and was imprisoned in Königstein Castle.

LEFT: A BMW R75 motorcycle crew in grey rubberised waterproof coats wait to board a coastal ferry at Narvik.

ABOVE: German troops in Norway armed with a 9mm MP34 Steyr-Solothurn SMG taken from Austrian police stocks in 1938.

About 40,000 Norwegians were imprisoned or sent to concentration camps, of whom about 2,000 including 700 Jews died. A further 500 Norwegians were killed or executed for resistance activities. Total war related civilian losses in the Norway during World War II were 8,000. Not all Norwegians resisted the German invaders. About 5,000 volunteers joined the Finnish Army and Waffen-SS and made up the 5th SS-Panzerdivision *"Wiking"* and the Waffen-SS Division *"Nordland"* which fought on the Eastern Front. For many men in occupied Europe combat against the USSR and Communism was a cause with which they could find sympathy.

The conquest of Denmark and Norway had cost the Germans 2,700 men, over 200 aircraft and a number of their most modern warships. The British had lost 4,400, the Norwegians 1,335 and the French and Poles 530. Though the Royal Navy had lost the aircraft carrier HMS *Glorious* and with it 1,500 men, the depletion of the *Kriegsmarine* that was a far smaller force would weigh significantly in the plans for the invasion of Britain that were only considered after the Fall of France in June 1940.

GERMAN NAVAL LOSSES IN NORWAY

SUNK
Blücher Heavy Cruiser
Karlsruhe Light Cruiser
Königsberg
Brummer Gunnery Training Ship

DESTROYERS
Anton Schmitt
Bernd von Arnim
Dieter von Roeder
Erich Geise
Erich Koellner
Georg Thiele
Hans Lüdemann
Herman Künne
Wilhelm Heidkamp
Wolfgang Zenker

U-BOATS
U1   U49
U13   U50
U22   U54
U44   U64

Albatros Torpedo Boat

TRANSPORTS
Antares
August Leonhardt
Bahia Castillo
Buenos Aires
Curityba
Florida
Friedenau
Hamm
Ionia
Kreta
Rio de Janeiro
Roda
Wigbert

DAMAGED
Lützow Pocket Battleship
Gneisenau Battle Cruiser
Scharnhorst
Bremse Gunnery Training Ship
Hipper Heavy Cruiser
Emden Light Cruiser

Smoke rises from sunken transports and warships following the Royal Navy attack in the Second Battle of Narvik.

INDEX